BATHROOM INSTALLATIONS

A Complete Guide

BATHROOM INSTALLATIONS

A Complete Guide

Planning, Managing and Completing Your Installation

Richard Moss

THE CROWOOD PRESS

First published in 2007 by
The Crowood Press Ltd
Ramsbury, Marlborough
Wiltshire SN8 2HR

www.crowood.com

British Library Cataloguing-in-Publication Data
A catalogue record for this book is available from the British Library.

ISBN 978 1 86126 919 5

Disclaimer
The author and the publisher do not accept any responsibility, in any manner whatsoever, for any error, or omission, nor any loss, damage, injury, adverse outcome or liability of any kind incurred as a result of the use of any of the information contained in this book, or reliance upon it. Readers are advised to seek professional advice relating to their particular bathroom, house, project and circumstances before embarking on any building or installation work.

Acknowledgements
The author would like to thank the following organisations for contributing images used in this book: Ripples; Mark Wilkinson Furniture; Members of Bathroom Manufacturer's Association; National Kitchen and Bath Association; Derby College Centre of Vocational Excellence; Jacuzzi UK; Ideal Standard UK Ltd; Hansgrohe UK.

   As products are regularly replaced or taken out of production, if you see a product that you would like to know more about, check the contributor's websites for the latest models available: www.ripples.ltd.uk; www.mwf.com; www.bathroom-association.org; www.nkba.org; www.jacuzziuk.com; www.ideal-standard.co.uk; www.hansgrohe.co.uk.

Line illustrations by Keith Field
Designed and typeset by Focus Publishing, Sevenoaks, Kent

Printed and bound in Singapore by Craft Print International Ltd

Contents

1   Introduction 7

2   Home and Family Considerations 14

3   Considering the Complete Bathroom 23

4   Baths 35

5   Sanitaryware 49

6   Brassware 68

7   Shower-Trays 78

8   Shower-Enclosures 89

9   Shower Controls and Kits 99

10 Frequently Asked Questions 119

Appendix: Industry Standards 128

Glossary 132

Useful Addresses 141

Index 143

CHAPTER 1

Introduction

The purpose of this book is to help you plan, choose and install a new bathroom in your home or introduce new products into your existing bathroom. It therefore covers complete or product partial replacement and the addition of entirely new facilities.

Starting with a little history to lay the foundations for any plans that you may make, the book then looks at a way to help you judge what your home, or family, needs in a new bathroom, before moving on to information on the individual bathroom elements with some installation guidance.

The reader is expected to have a good level of installation skills and the book strongly suggests that specific skilled help is called upon where necessary, especially when dealing with construction, electrical and plumbing skills.

In the past, the bathroom in British homes tended to be a functional room, supplied and installed by the local plumber, who often had little understanding of life-style needs or interior design. Nowadays the bathroom has changed dramatically and – influenced by central heating, which brought warmer living environments, and by broader travel horizons, which introduced Continental design trends – bathrooms in British homes are now a place to linger and to be enjoyed.

Over the past five years in particular, the bathroom is the room that features most on the TV makeover programmes and in glossy home interest magazines. It has become a room that adds investment value to homes and adds to the status of the home-owner – everyone visiting the house, visits the bathroom sooner or later. Consequently, the bathroom has risen to the top of most home-owner's wish-list of rooms to be revamped.

The bathroom has also grown in status as the populations of European countries grow older – in the next forty years there will be an extra forty-seven million people over the age of sixty, living in Europe. Those people will want to live in their own homes and the bathroom, with its washing and toilet facilities, will be crucial in allowing them to do that as they grow more infirm. Current home design is already geared to being more practical for older and less able people, with its wider doors and easier access, plus its ground-floor cloakroom and growing numbers of *en suite* facilities. Such facilities can only grow in significance and in importance in affecting future life-styles and future house values.

Bathrooms are made up of a series of product-types manufactured from a variety of materials – ceramics, glass, metals, wood and acrylics being archetypal – this makes the installation of a bathroom a multi-skilled project. Plumbing skills, installation skills and decoration skills are all needed

OPPOSITE: Bathrooms are smaller in Britain than in the rest of the Western World, but like Europe and the USA, we are demanding more bathrooms in our homes and need make no compromise on comfort and style. (Ideal Standard)

Top tip

Water is the opposite to money – a little can go an awfully long way!

---

when fitting a modern bathroom. The most important of these being plumbing, because leaking water can do a terrific amount of damage to the decoration and fabric of a home, if not properly controlled.

Readers should always be careful to follow manufacturer's installation instructions and to employ specialist skills, such as plumbers, tilers and electricians, as appropriate. On larger jobs concerning alterations to the fabric of the building, a specialist designer or architect needs to be consulted. In the case of alterations to the water and heating supply within the home, a specialist plumbing and/or heating engineer may be required. There are many such professionals available and readers can find associations that cover all skills at the end of the book.

AIM OF THE BOOK

The aim of this book is to provide general guidance and knowledge for people, who are planning to refurbish their bathroom. The reader may decide to pass full responsibility to a commissioned supplier, in which case this book will be an invaluable reference work that will enable the householder to shadow the professional and understand better, what their supplier is proposing. Alternatively, readers may be DIY enthusiasts, who require guidance on planning and managing the installation. The book acts as a guide for this purpose and will provide links to appropriate organisations and their web-sites.

HISTORY'S EFFECT ON DESIGN

There is some architectural evidence from 3,000 years ago indicating that homes in the Indus Valley (modern-day Iraq) were built with their own drainage pipes leading out of the house. A thousand years later, the Romans brought the idea and the technology of crude sewers, along with central heating, to Britain. Notwithstanding this, toileting facilities in the home only resurfaced in the middle to late Victorian era and, along with central heating, was not installed in the majority of UK homes for a further hundred years.

In the 1850s, the average life expectancy for a working family living in Great Britain was thirty-five years; by the beginning of the twentieth century that

had grown to forty years. Today, cleaner water through more hygienic toileting and proper sewers, along with warmer homes and a better diet, have all contributed to stretching that average life expectancy closer to twice the Victorian's age. In the developed world, having high standards of sanitation and health are no longer optional considerations, they are both expected and demanded. In fact most UK families take it for granted that having a bathroom in our homes is a long-established part of British living, but it is not.

As recently as the 1960s – and in more remote parts of the country, a decade or so later – there were homes in the UK that had no bathing or toileting facilities in them; in some cases the toilet was situated in a small brick-built or timber shed, often with a corrugated-iron roof, called a privy. Positioned a short walk away from the home, or row of homes, the inside of a typical 'privy' featured a plank of wood fixed above a shallow trench, one, two and sometimes three six-inch diameter holes cut in the plank formed the toilet seats.

The privy usually had one door and consideration for the neighbours consisted of a bucket of lime to drop in the trench after use and a nail to carry the squares of

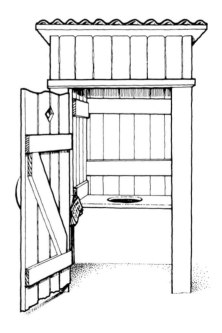

A typical privy – this one is a single-seater!

newspaper. That is a real scenario that would be totally unacceptable today, but it is a good illustration of the rapid and dramatic change in our attitudes to the bathroom over two or three generations.

The typical late-Victorian and Edwardian 'back-to-backs' and terrace-houses, which still exist in many industrial towns, allowed slightly better facilities; these homes sported a flushing toilet in an outhouse down the yard. It was freezing cold in winter but a degree of privacy had been introduced.

The Old Tin Bath

No matter what kind of toilet the home had – privy or out-house – in most homes taking a bath was a weekly affair using a tin bath that was brought into the house every Friday from its storage place hanging in the shed; it was strategically positioned in the warmest place in the home, in front of the range, for everyone in the family to share.

In the second-half of the twentieth century, toilets were brought into every home, in a tiny room that sat next to an equally tiny and separate room with a fixed and plumbed-in bath. There are millions of homes still like this and millions more, where the dividing wall between the two rooms has been removed to make one larger room that holds both the toilet and the bath. When it comes to frequency of using bathrooms, there have also been dramatic changes, in just three generations. My grandfather's family bathed once a week and as school kids many of the baby-boomer generation still followed that pattern, although the tin bath had been replaced by a permanently fixed bath.

A typical day now could see the family taking a shower every morning (we tell ourselves that it is to refresh us and wake ourselves up) and taking a bath every evening (to wash away the stress of a working day). In fact there is growing evidence that the shower is also becoming more sophisticated as part of the 'pampering process' with multiple jets and a number of effects, from steam to chromotherapy, being included in the features on modern super-showers.

Such a rapid speed of change over two or three generations has been accompanied by a variety of designs and fashions. The avocado colouring that was the norm in the 1970s is 'wouldn't-be-seen-dead-with' today and the pseudo-Victorian styling that was

Award-winning London design team Luke Pearson and Tom Lloyd, won their reputation designing for Virgin Atlantic and Westminster Council; here they check out the detail in their latest bathroom assignment, a walk-in shower system. (Trevi Showers)

the high-fashion of the late 1980s and early 1990s are no longer as popular as they were. Fashions in furniture or soft-furnishings have been around for centuries but bathroom fashions are a relatively new phenomenon and are being enthusiastically embraced by today's top designers.

CURRENT FASHION TRENDS

Like many aspects of British homes, the bathroom therefore has become subject to fashion and, if current trends do have a set theme, it is the eclectic nature of design in the first decade of the twenty-first century – there are no rules. Home-owners want to stamp their own individuality on their homes, but at the same time they realise that a home is an important investment and if the interior design choices are too drastic, they will at best 'date' the interior and at worst make the property difficult to sell.

Thus home-owners have plenty of choice to do whatever pleases them in terms of design, but the desire to maintain the sale value of their home imposes discipline. In any event, all bathroom refurbishments in the UK are controlled by the, generally, limited size of British bathrooms, most of which have the same floor area as a king-sized bed!

If you live in an older house, that still has the separate bathroom and toilet, you can challenge the idea of removing that dividing wall between the two small rooms, but you need to ask yourself is it a good thing, or will you be acting in haste, just to follow a trend? Is it better to retain two rooms thus allowing the bath and the toilet to be used separately? Assessing the current and future needs of your family will help you make your decisions, as will the planning guide in Chapter 2.

Current design trends are moving away from the neo-Victorian and toward more simple designs – often described by words such as 'minimalist'. Although it should be noted that the more extreme minimalism is now a 'passed' trend and the current mood is for softer, more 'human' designs but without the clutter of Victoriana. 'Simplicity' and 'clean' incorporating gentle curves are now the key words. White is the colour, carpets are 'out' and floor tiling, laminate flooring and smooth surfaces are coming 'in' (with support from under-floor heating to warm the standing surface). In taps and brass fittings, 'gold' has almost disappeared and 'chromium' is universal. Fashion has even caught up with heating radiators, with some very sculptural shapes now being available, as well as co-ordinating storage units that mirror the shapes or materials of the bathroom fixtures.

British home-owners and their families not only wash and bathe much more often than their grandparents, but for very different reasons they have embraced the shower as an alternative or a supplement to the bath. In terms of speed and, in some cases, greater

Showing how fashion trends swing, here we see Royal Designer for Industry, Robin Levien, testing one of his studio's latest bath designs. It could be argued that this is a modern version of the old tin-bath, or perhaps a development of the cast-iron Victorian roll top. Robin's bath is produced from a cast-resin material that is a modern version of the old cast-iron. (Sottini)

refreshment, the shower is more convenient. A recent study in Scandinavia found that teenagers shower several times per day and much more often than their parents. Similarly their parents bathing habits are completely different from those of their own parents. The study found that the reason for teenagers' multi-showering was peer pressure to smell good. Indeed, body odour these days, particularly amongst sporty and energetic youngsters, is totally unacceptable. In terms of the attitudes we hold, we have taken a huge step away from the communal odours of the shared privy.

One sure thing about fashion though, is that it always swings back towards earlier styles, although with a quite different interpretation. It is a case for 'the same as it was but different', not real Victorian, but much more efficient and modern 'Victorian'. I'm afraid that means you cannot retain that old avocado suite and wait for it to come back 'in' because the next avocado will be a significantly different shade of green and your home will still be dated if you have not changed it.

THE EFFECT OF LEGISLATION ON BATHROOM FASHION

Since 1998, legislation has decreed that new homes have to be built with a second toilet, in a cloakroom, on the ground floor, so as to cater for the requirements of less ambulant people, who are unable to, or who have a real difficulty in, walking upstairs to the toilet. Over the same period, fashion has decreed that homes need a third toilet, accompanied by a bath or maybe a shower, as an *en suite* to the master bedroom. Some homes have a bathroom for every bedroom, and in some homes the bath has now become part of the bedroom furniture.

New home design is changing and the government is encouraging the construction of new homes that have a 'smaller imprint' on the environment' in terms of both land used and energy consumption.

Building contractors are being encouraged by planners to squeeze more houses on to the same plot of land and this is already prompting the construction of three-storey housing, which, to remain within the Disability Discrimination Act, will

RIGHT: A reversal of the trend, which has seen us turning two rooms into one, this bathroom has turned one room into two – to create a master bathroom and an en suite shower room. The corner toilet in the bathroom and the basin in the en suite help to save space. In a typical home installation, it is likely that there would be a window in the main room, which could be over the basin or in place of the radiator (whichever was the external wall); in such a case, under-floor heating could be utilized. (Ideal Standard)

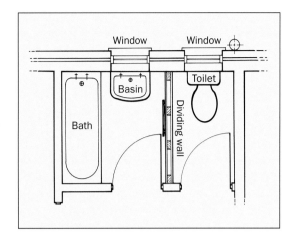

Separate bathroom and toilet divided by a stud-wall.

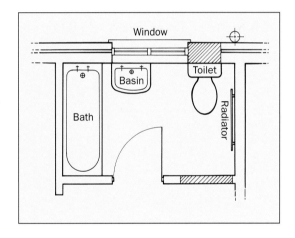

Many people have removed the dividing wall to make one larger room, but is that the right thing to do?

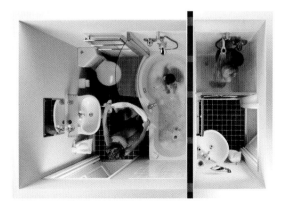

require a toilet on each floor, which is sensible given that people, on average, live longer than they used to, but is likely to lead to even smaller bathrooms.

For people living in houses with just one bathroom, these trends become vital considerations when they want to resell their homes – does the prospective buyer want an older home with just one bathroom, or a newly built home with three or more bathrooms? Finding space for additional bathing and toileting facilities will become much more significant in the replacement-homes market.

The way we use our bathrooms has also changed completely, what we expect of our bathrooms has changed dramatically and with that there is a probability that every family has its own unique bathing habits. We all want our bathrooms to match our individual life-styles. It is no longer just a functional room dedicated to health and hygiene; it has become a haven of status, style and fashion.

A downstairs cloakroom offers easier access for anyone to whom climbing stairs is a challenge. (Ideal Standard)

A modern version of the Victorian wash-stand. The originals often had a wooden stand upon which sat a free-standing porcelain basin and a ewer for fresh water. Things have changed a lot in the past century, but sometimes there is a real similarity in the look. (Ceramica Dolimite)

Over the last three generations, the bathroom for many families has become the place where they can refresh themselves, a place to escape from the din of family life, a place where they can pamper themselves with oils and unguents and massaging bubbles, a place in which to really relax or even to have fun. For many decades it was generally accepted that the kitchen was the heart of the home, today the bathroom has become the home's soul.

Before we move on and move away from legislation it is important to be aware of the concerns that are arising over using water efficiently in the home. As you would expect, bathrooms are a key focus for government and standards-setting bodies; climate change and drought are very modern threats and so using water efficiently needs to come into our thinking when designing a new bathroom.

CHAPTER 2

Home and Family Considerations

The starting point of any bathroom installation is deciding what bathing and toileting facilities you and your family are likely to need over the life of the bathroom, which research shows to be around fifteen years. Once that decision is made, you then need to design the room that will satisfy what you want. Planning, managing and completing a bathroom installation to suit your life-style is the object of this book and the following survey guide will give readers a good idea on where to start to create their own room design, or to brief their bathroom designer on the needs of their family and their tastes.

RATE YOUR EXISTING OR PLANNED BATHROOM

We start with an easy guide to help you to 'rate' the bathroom facilities that are already in your home and to give you an idea about additional bathroom features that you can enjoy while you live there. Equally, this guide helps you to think about facilities that would attract potential buyers if you are looking to install an attractive bathroom that will add value to your property, when you want to sell it.

PLANNING YOUR NEW BATHROOM

Filling in the survey gives you a template of what your bathroom needs to deliver for you and your family – in terms of fitting a new bathroom, one of the most important consideration is availability of hot water; if you have a condensing boiler, that will be no problem.

Does Your House Have Enough Hot Water?

Most pre-1990 houses use hot water typically stored in a 900 × 450mm diameter indirect cylinder that will hold around 90ltr of water; tanks in newer houses store 115 or 230ltr. You need to ensure you will have enough water to meet your showering needs. It is no good fitting a multi-jet or a power-shower that delivers 15ltr of water per minute if you only have 90ltr of hot water in your storage tank and you like to wallow in a powerful shower for five or six minutes – especially if another family member is queuing to take their shower straight after you. To check the capacity of your storage tank, get the advice of a professional plumber. To fit a larger tank is a job for a professional plumber.

Decide on the Room and do the Research

The other pre-requisite, before you begin any room plans, is to decide whether you are simply going to refit the existing bathroom, whether you are going

---

The 'Rate Your Bathroom' Survey

This is for you to use as a guide to identifying your bathroom needs. It is based on the work that I have done with the USA's, National Kitchen and Bath Association (NKBA) and the British, Bathroom Manufacturers Association (BMA). It is intended as an *aide-mémoir* to the factors you may wish to consider before planning your new bathroom.

RATE YOUR BATHROOM

SET YOUR DESIGN OBJECTIVES

Note three features of your current bathroom that you LIKE the most.
1. _____
2. _____
3. _____

Note three features of your current bathroom that you DISLIKE the most.
1. _____
2. _____
3. _____

Note three new features that you 'MUST HAVE' in your new bathroom.
1. _____
2. _____
3. _____

Note which single feature you 'WOULD LOVE TO HAVE' in your new bathroom but don't think you can have?
1. _____

STRUCTURAL

	Yes	No
Is your hot water supply adequate?	☐	☐
If not:		
– should you change the storage tank?	☐	☐
– should you change your boiler?	☐	☐
Is your existing bathroom big enough?	☐	☐
– If not can you extend it?	☐	☐
– Or, can you move it to another room?	☐	☐
Is there need and room in your house for added facilities?	☐	☐
– Do you need a downstairs cloakroom?	☐	☐
– Do you want an en suite?	☐	☐
Does the bathroom window let in enough light?	☐	☐

THE FAMILY AND THE HOME

	Yes	No
How many people use the bathroom in your home? _____		
Is there an alternative bathroom when busy?	☐	☐
Is one (or more) of the family ever waiting to use the toilet?	☐	☐
Is one of the family ever waiting to use the washing?	☐	☐
Is there an older person in the family?	☐	☐
Is there a disabled person in the family?	☐	☐

FACILITIES

Bathing

	Yes	No
Would you like a bigger bath?	☐	☐
Would you like a 'double' bath?	☐	☐
Would you like a 'whirlpool' bath?	☐	☐
Do you feel safe stepping into and out of the bath?	☐	☐
Do you want a shower over the bath?	☐	☐
Where will you want your soap-holders? _____		
Where would you like to position the rail for bath-towels? _____		
What kind of bath-filler do you want? _____		

Shower

	Yes	No
Do you want a separate enclosure?	☐	☐
Do you want a 'wellness' shower (body-jets, steam etc)	☐	☐
Do you want a wet-room?	☐	☐

continued overleaf

	Yes	No
If you already have a shower		
– is the spray at the right height?	☐	☐
– do you feel safe using the shower?	☐	☐
– does your shower have safety glass?	☐	☐
– would you like a more powerful shower?	☐	☐
– would you like a seat in your shower?	☐	☐
– is you shower glass easy to clean?	☐	☐
– are the soap holders at a convenient height?	☐	☐
Where would you like the rail for shower-towels?	_____	

Washbasin

	Yes	No
Is it at a convenient height?	☐	☐
Would you like a double washbasin?	☐	☐
Are the taps easy to operate?	☐	☐
Would you like water-efficient taps?	☐	☐
Where would you like the rail for basin-towels?	_____	

Toilet

	Yes	No
Is the toilet in the right position for you?	☐	☐
Is your toilet the correct height for you?	☐	☐
Would you like a water-efficient toilet?	☐	☐
Are the roll-holders in the most convenient place?	☐	☐
Would you like a bidet?	☐	☐
Does a member of your family have a special need when using the bath, toilet, washbasin or taps?	☐	☐

STORAGE

	Yes	No
Do you have enough storage for:		
Hair gels and shaving gels?	☐	☐
Shampoos and soaps?	☐	☐
Bath additives?	☐	☐
Razors?	☐	☐
Tooth cleaners (brushes, pastes, floss)?	☐	☐
Towels and flannels?	☐	☐
Toilet rolls?	☐	☐
Bleaches and cleaners?	☐	☐

DECORATION

	Yes	No
What style of bathroom would you like?		
Feng Shui	☐	☐
Loft	☐	☐
Modern	☐	☐
Minimalist	☐	☐
Other	_____	
Does your existing décor look dated?	☐	☐
Does your bathroom feel comfortable?	☐	☐
Do you like the colour of the bathroom fixtures?	☐	☐
Is there adequate lighting?	☐	☐
Is there adequate ventilation?	☐	☐
What flooring do you want?		
Carpet	☐	☐
Ceramic tiles	☐	☐
Laminate	☐	☐
Other: sheet flooring, Amtico, Karndean?	_____	

How to Choose the Style

Research the styles you like by buying home interest magazines, visiting showrooms, visiting friends with new bathrooms and collecting brochures from showrooms.

to extend it, or whether you are going to knock through, or use an adjacent larger room, such as an existing bedroom. Again some of the construction skills required can easily be tackled by a competent DIY enthusiast. For guidance on building a stud partition wall or replacing a wooden window, refer to

Mike Lawrence's book *The DIY Guide to Doors, Windows and Joinery*, published by Crowood.

While every house can be different, the vast majority of installations will follow the patterns shown in the following floor plans. You will need to research the products available but it is safe to say that whatever you want, there will be one available. Do send for brochures and spend a month or so looking through them. You may want short projection (300mm) basins for a downstairs cloakroom or space-saving toilet designs or speciality shower-baths that double the usage from your floor space – read through the sections on individual products before you begin to plan.

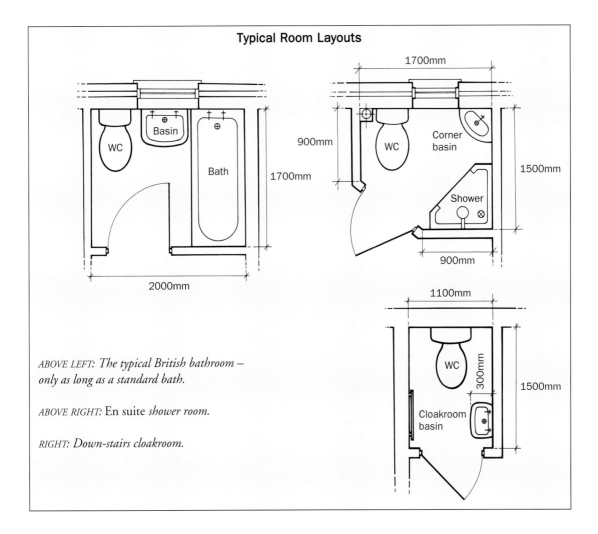

Typical Room Layouts

ABOVE LEFT: The typical British bathroom – only as long as a standard bath.

ABOVE RIGHT: En suite *shower room.*

RIGHT: Down-stairs cloakroom.

Minimum Space Requirements

With the likelihood of readers and their families enjoying a longer lifespan over the coming decades, and the importance of bathroom facilities in enabling us to continue to live an independent life in our own homes, many pundits are suggesting that it is time for the bathroom to shed its epithet of The Smallest Room and grow into A Much Larger Room, to allow for additional space required by aids, such as wheel-chairs, hoists and transfer shelves, and also for carers to have the room to help their charges. To plan an appropriate Big Bathroom in existing homes would probably mean moving the current bathroom into an unused bedroom.

Currently the British Standards recommend the following spaces to be allowed to gain safe access to bathroom equipment and to give room for drying and dressing – BSi calls these areas 'activity spaces'.

A bath requires an activity space of 700 × 1,100mm, a shower-enclosure needs an activity space 700 × 900mm, while a washbasin needs an activity area of 700 × 1,000mm, which reduces

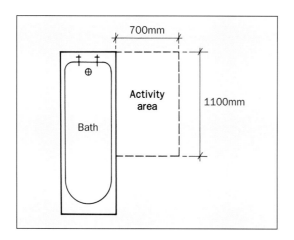

A standard sized bath, showing the activity area.

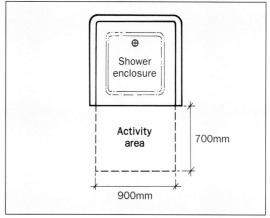

A shower, enclosed on three sides, requires an activity area 700 × 900mm. This area is sufficient for drying but a nearby dressing area of 1,200 × 900mm would also be expected.

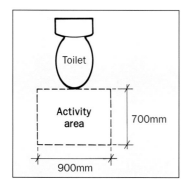

A toilet requires an activity area of 600 × 800mm.

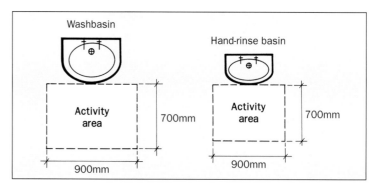

A washbasin, requires an activity area of 700 × 1000mm, which reduces to 600 × 800mm for a cloakroom basin or hand-rinse basin.

to 600 × 800mm for a cloakroom basin or hand-rinse basin. The toilet (or WC) requires an activity area 600 × 800mm.

Draw the Floor Plan

Once you have decided what facilities you would like, and whether you are going to leave the bathroom where it is or use another room, the next key step is to draw up a scaled floor-plan. This can be drawn up simply on graph paper – a scale of 1:20 is what most bathroom designers use. At this stage there is no need to consider décor, this initial plan is to tell you what facilities will fit in the room and how you can position the facilities to best suit your lifestyle. There are a number of ways to get help with this planning; for example, there are a number of simple CAD facilities on the internet and a more comprehensive design service is often offered by bathroom showrooms.

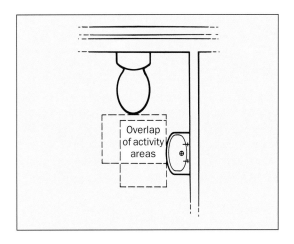

Overlapping of activity areas is expected – it is rare for any two adjacent bathroom appliances to be used simultaneously. This diagram shows the overlap between the activity areas for the toilet and the basin.

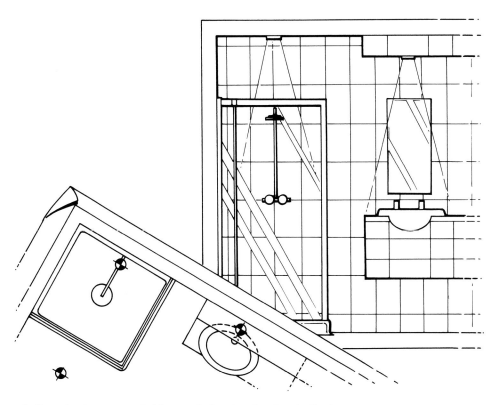

This simple floor plan is accompanied by a wall elevation showing the furniture, washbasin and shower-enclosure. (Ripples)

WHERE TO BUY AND WHAT SERVICE TO EXPECT

Bathrooms can be purchased from a number of different sources, which offer a variety of price ranges and services, which include:

- architects or interior design practices;
- independent bathroom specialist showrooms;
- plumbing companies or independent plumbers;
- builders' merchants, some of which have full showrooms;
- DIY stores;
- the internet.

Architects and Interior Design Practices

For a major home project that includes bathrooms, the architect and/or interior designer can give you super advice and project manage the job for you. These kinds of businesses specialize in the design for the whole home: for architects, that is as a designer of exterior and interior spaces and shapes, plus construction supervisor; for interior designers, that is usually as a room designer and often with a focus on décor. Both interior designers and architects charge for the design work that they do. Neither of them specialize, as a general rule, on bathroom planning, so if you are looking to focus only on the bathroom, they can be an expensive option.

Independent Bathroom Specialists

There are a number of independent bathroom show-rooms, throughout the UK, that specialize in the supply of bathroom products, many of these have a room-planning service and can provide a good installation team. Some of these businesses are members of the Independent Bathroom Specialists Association (IBSA); these usually offer advice on all of the latest bathroom products and trends, and have room-set displays where readers can touch and feel and, in some cases, try out the bathrooms before purchasing. These independent retailers normally have show-rooms that are situated in 'high street' style shopping areas.

IBSA members normally offer a room-design service that is often free of charge, many of them can plan and carry out installation projects. Sometimes these businesses employ their own installation teams, although it is more common for them to work with a chosen number of installation teams. IBSA members

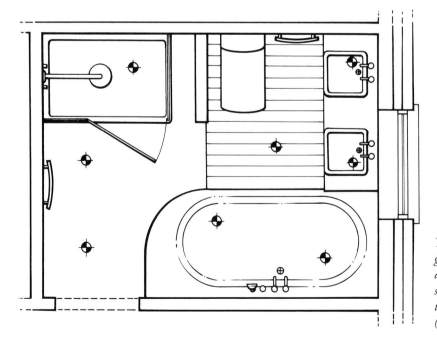

The UK has many good bathroom designers for those who seek layouts that match their individuality. (Ripples)

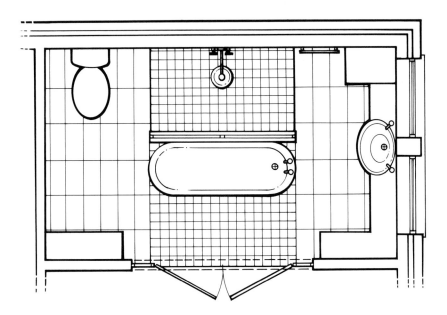

This imaginative bathroom design is actually an en suite that opens up from the bedroom and can be kept private by closing the doors or made more inclusive for the person using the bath, by folding the doors back. The shower positioned behind the bath is also an unusual feature. The plan was devised by one of the designers at Ripples, which is an IBSA member. (Ripples)

offer a full warranty against work done, which can be valuable for anyone who is a little nervous about installing a new bathroom.

For a list of IBSA members visit: www.ibsa.org.uk

There are also around 300 showrooms in the UK that are members of the Kitchen and Bathroom Specialists Association (KBSA); these are mainly independent showrooms, some of which have only kitchen displays but some also include bathroom displays and offer a design and installation service. Members details can be found on: www.kbsa.co.uk

Not all bathroom specialists belong to an association, however, and there are many more excellent showrooms throughout the UK that offer a design and installation service; the sensible way to check out their competence is to examine some of their past work.

Plumbers

Most plumbing companies and independent plumbers will fit a new bathroom. Some of these plumbers will also supply the products – their source would be the local plumbing or builder's merchant. Those that do not supply, will invariably advise you on what bathroom products to buy and where to go to buy them.

The best listing of plumbers in England and Wales is available at: www.iphe.org.uk, while for plumbers in Scotland or Northern Ireland look at: www.snipef.org

Other than via these web-sites, the best place to look for plumbers are the telephone directories or by taking advice from acquaintances that you trust, who have recently had their bathroom installed. Plumbers are often accused of being less interested in the overall room design than the others – they are practical people, some of whom only want to refit exactly what was there before, but these days plumbers are more design savvy and they should not be ignored as a source of design and fit suppliers.

Builders' Merchants

Many builders' merchants now have bathroom show-rooms, in fact the way a typical builder's merchant sells bathrooms starts at its trade counter, where its trade customers (and in some cases consumers) can go with a list of the bathroom components that they want and carry them away with them. The trade counters generally sell lower- to middle-priced bathroom products.

In some cases the merchants may have floor areas set out, with basic displays, so that the plumber can take his customer to see a full bathroom suite. Again, the tendency is for the mid-priced ranges to be on display. More and more these days, builders' and plumbers' merchants will also have luxury show-rooms, which display a variety of bathroom schemes and products. This level of display is normally tiled and decorated and often the middle- to upper-priced ranges are on show.

DIY Store

As you would expect, the major DIY stores sell to the mass market and so they normally carry products with the lowest prices. In the past few years it seems that the DIY stores that cover the whole house have the most reliable level of service, while the DIY stores that specialize in (say) home electrical or home furniture have shown a tendency to move in and out of the bathroom market. You can get a low price from a DIY store, but you will need to know what you want and how to install it.

Internet

The internet can be used for two main purposes: to research what is available or, to buy. As with all industries now, there is a tremendous body of knowledge about bathrooms on the internet. A good starting place to find what you need is available on: www.bathroom-association.org, which has links to the majority of manufacturers working in the UK and plenty of further advice on bathroom design and installation. Buying from the web is becoming a safer option but the usual care must be taken.

There is a stringent code of standards for the UK and a growing focus for applying them, especially in the fields of water efficiency – or on subjects such as ensuring shower-screens and enclosures are made from safety-glass.

DO-IT-YOURSELF CONSIDERATIONS

The bathroom can appear to be a very complex do-it-yourself project in terms of the skills needed for a full installation – you may need the skills of a plumber, an electrician, a builder, a decorator and a tiler. Much of the practical work is logical and mechanical, however, and with care and application, within the skills of most experienced DIY enthusiasts.

Of course, where external skills are needed or are demanded by law, they must be scheduled into your project management plan. Another important consideration, of course, is to plan to supply the necessary facilities, while the work is being done!

CHAPTER 3

Considering the Complete Bathroom

This chapter takes a brief look at preparatory work relating to the room into which you intend to install the bathroom and offers a few ideas that may stretch your thinking. It is important that, in the case where you may want to completely reposition bathroom equipment or fit additional elements to your bathroom, you employ professional advice that relates to your particular installation. Both the age of your property and its location will have a bearing on the type of water delivery and sewage removal system that applies to your home. Another variable may come in the changes to building regulations relating to water usage and home services, which are under consideration at the time this is being written.

CONSULT

With the factors that could impact in a bathroom installation in mind, we will discuss: stop-taps, to enable you to safely cut off the water supply while you are working; water supply systems, to enable you to chose a tap that matches your system; water pressures, so that you can be sure that the shower system that you want will work on your system; positioning of pipe lengths, so that the physics of your bathroom work properly; and, finally, capacity of water stored, so that you can be sure you will not run short.

In all of these cases, it is wise to consult a professional plumber on all but the simplest mechanical changes. In fact, in some areas of work on the services in houses, the laws are changing and you may be obliged by law to consult a competent person and perhaps inform your local building inspectorate.

STOP-VALVES

Modern homes have a number of means to restrict the flow of water, some of which apply to houses of all ages. There are two stop-valves, or stop-taps, which cut off the complete flow of water into your house. One is located outside the property and it cuts off the supply to the service pipe to the house from the Water Company's water main; you would not expect to have to cut off your water supply using this first stop-valve and will have to call the water company if such a need should occur, but it is still worthwhile ensuring that you know where it is and that you have the water company's contact number available in case of an emergency. The second stop-valve servicing your home will be positioned within 600mm of the place where the main water service pipe enters your home; this is usually under the kitchen sink.

Isolation valves are also fitted throughout the water supply system, the variety of ages and systems in British houses makes it essential that you know how to isolate the water supply before working on the water system – again, if you do not fully understand it, consult a professional.

UNDERSTANDING PLUMBING SYSTEMS

Your home could have a direct system or an indirect system of supply. A direct system supplies cold water at mains pressure to all of the points where it is needed, while an indirect system supplies cold water to the kitchen tap only, and stores other cold water in a tank, usually situated in the roof space.

Before specifying particular taps or showers it is necessary to establish what type of hot-water system exists in the property. The UK is pretty much alone in Europe in having, traditionally, fitted low-pressure or unbalanced water systems. It is a throwback to the pioneering work of the Victorian's, which relied on air gaps rather than mechanical valves to ensure there was no cross-infection into the supply system. This is gradually changing with the advent of direct-supply combination boilers. The significance to a new bathroom installation mainly relates to the type of tap or shower valve that is used. Basically, taps designed for mainland Europe are intended for high-pressure systems and will not work properly on a typical UK low-pressure system.

Low-Pressure Systems

Hot and Cold Gravity-Fed Water Systems

This is the typical arrangement that is used in older properties. The cold-water supply that enters your home from the water main usually has plenty of pressure. This water comes into the house at mains pressure and is fed directly to the kitchen tap. A quick check of initial mains pressure can be seen by turning the cold supply from the kitchen tap on full and observing the flow of water.

The mains water is also piped directly to a cold-water cistern or tank, which is located in the loft. The tank feeds the rest of the domestic cold-water supply and also the cold-water supply to the hot-water cylinder. The height of this tank influences the cold- and hot-water pressure to the whole house.

Some older houses still store the cold water in a galvanized water tank that is below the roof-space, which could have an adverse effect on the pressure, or head, of water feeding a shower. If this is the case, before fitting out a new bathroom, check the tank for wear (galvanized tanks do wear out) and consider fitting a new, properly insulated, plastic tank into the roof space.

In this system, as with the other low-pressure systems, the hot-water cylinder or 'hot tank' is usually situated in an airing cupboard and stores hot water that feeds the domestic hot-water supply system.

Hot and Cold Pumped System

As with the hot and cold gravity-fed water system, this system has a cold-water tank, normally located in the loft, feeding both the domestic cold-water supply and also the cold-water supply to the hot-water storage tank. A pump is then fitted to provide a higher volume of water.

Gravity-Fed Hot-Water and Mains-Fed Cold-Water System

This system differs from the hot and cold gravity system because the supply to all of the cold taps comes directly from the mains and so is at mains pressure; in almost all cases this will create an imbalance in pressures. Pressure imbalance normally greater than 5:1 will require a pressure-reducing valve to be fitted on the dominant supply. This is particularly important if you are planning to use a modern mixer tap, where the water flow mixes before it leaves the spout. If you are not fully competent or knowledgeable in this area, use a plumber. As with other low-pressure systems, this system also operates from a cold-water tank and is normally located in the loft, feeding the cold water required for the hot-water tank.

High-Pressure Systems

Mains-Fed Hot-Water System

These hot-water systems provide hot water on demand, as and when required. Combination (or Combi) boilers and multi-point boilers, heat mains cold water instantaneously as it flows through a heat-exchange unit within the boiler. Operating pressure for these units is usually between 0.5 and 10bar. Within this pressure range, sufficient water must flow through the boiler when a tap or shower is turned on, in order to activate a flow sensor in the boiler. When activated, the flow sensor initiates heat transfer to the domestic hot-water circuit. There is a minimum flow to activate the water-heating process – check the boiler instructions.

Any system providing a mains pressure supply, relies on the flow and pressure of water entering the property. A product may boast, for example, 30ltr/min flow rate at 3bar pressure, but if the supply to the property is inadequate and can only muster,

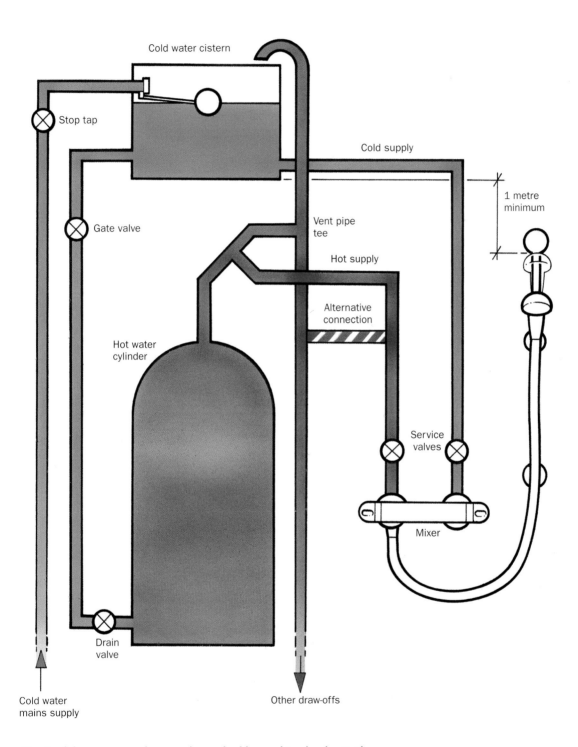

Cold water cistern

Stop tap

Cold supply

1 metre
minimum

Gate valve

Vent pipe
tee

Hot supply

Alternative
connection

Hot water
cylinder

Service
valves

Mixer

Drain
valve

Cold water
mains supply

Other draw-offs

Gravity-fed water system showers – hot and cold – need 1m head or 0.1bar.

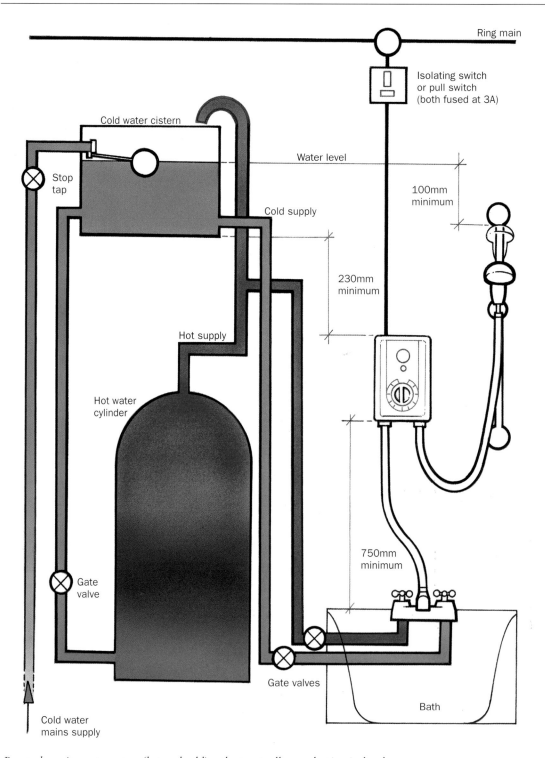

Ring main

Isolating switch
or pull switch
(both fused at 3A)

Cold water cistern

Water level

100mm
minimum

Stop
tap

Cold supply

230mm
minimum

Hot supply

Hot water
cylinder

750mm
minimum

Gate
valve

Gate valves

Bath

Cold water
mains supply

Pumped gravity water system (hot and cold) – the pump allows reduction in head.

say, 15ltr at 1bar, then this is all that will be achieved. Figures quoted against products are indicative of their potential based on an adequate supply.

Hot-Water Storage Capacity

Modern homes have a main bathroom, a downstairs' cloakroom and, usually, an *en suite* bath or shower-room (or two), so a queue for the bathroom is becoming much rarer. These days, we have enough washing facilities but there may be a question as to whether or not we have enough water.

In a recent survey amongst bathroom manufacturers, one of the major complaints following the installation of a new bathroom was running out of hot water before everyone in the family had taken their bath or shower. Whether you are fitting your

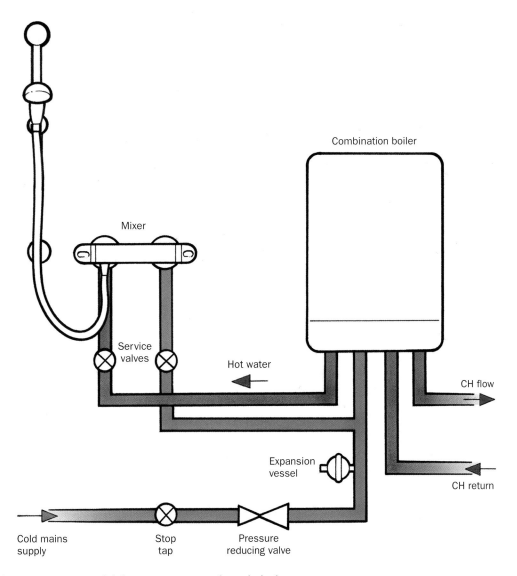

High-pressure, or mains-fed, hot-water system with combi boiler.

Make Sure You Have Enough Hot Water

This is not normally an issue with the newer condenser boilers, which heat the mains water on demand. It is, however, an important consideration for the unbalanced or gravity-fed water system that exist in the vast majority of our homes.

---

own new bathroom, or you are employing an installer, there are a few things you need to know, to ensure this does not happen to you.

To get a rough rule-of-thumb on the volume of water that you need, consider the peak times when demand is at its highest. i.e. mornings getting ready for work/college/school and in the evening when everyone is preparing for a night out – how many baths/showers does your family need?

The size of the hot-water tank in a gravity-fed system will depend on the supply of water that the home requires. For a typical home that is between 115 and 230ltr. A shower tends to flow at 9ltr/min, so if you spend five minutes in the shower, then you will need 45ltr of water, a significant proportion of which will come from the hot tank. If you have a multi-valve and/or powered shower, the volumes will be much higher. If you have a family member who likes to dwell in the shower, then there could be a problem for the person following.

The volume of water taken by a bath varies but let's say that a typical bath takes between 180 and 225ltr up to the overflow – again a large portion of that water will be hot. For families that refuse to share bath-water, then taking a number of baths or mixtures of bath and shower can sometimes strain the system.

Water Pressure

Water pressure impacts on the bathroom at the points of water delivery, affecting the speed at which a toilet cistern will refill or the flow of water from a tap, which can make bath filling a slow process, but in the main it impacts on the flow from a shower-head. Water pressure in the home is referred to as 'bar' and many showers and taps will refer to requiring 'n' bar to operate properly.

Bar is measured as the height (or head) of water above the point at which it will be delivered. So, if the bottom of the cold water storage tank is 2m above the shower-spray from which the water will be delivered, that is called a 2m-head of water. One 'bar' of water requires 10m of 'head'; so, 2m of head is 0.2bar – the greater the distance (head), the greater the pressure.

Water Temperature

The temperature at which we store hot water and deliver hot water to a bath, shower or basin is under scrutiny just now. In fact changes to the regulations were made in Scotland in 2006 and at the time of writing, changes are being considered for the rest of Britain.

The changes stem from a need to store hot water above 60°C to kill any bacteria in the system, while delivering the water at a safe temperature from the taps. For many years, building standards have required hospitals and care-homes to use thermostatic mixer valves (TMV) for this purpose and it looks as though those regulations are about to spread into our homes. Be aware of any building regulations or bye laws that impact on your installation and be ready to install a TMV to the bath and/or basin in

Example of an under-bath thermostat. (The Blue Book)

your new bathroom, if required. TMVs have been used in shower controls for many years. Some people, who like to soak in the bath and top up the hot supply, are arguing against having thermostatically restricted temperatures because there would only be 'warm' rather than 'hot' water available for their top-ups, but the case for protecting children or other vulnerable people from the threat of scalding is very strong.

READYING THE ROOM

This book concentrates on the installation of the core bathroom elements: sanitaryware, baths, showers and brassware. For advice on structural work take a look at *The DIY Guide to Doors, Windows and Joinery, Masonry and Plastering* and *Wiring and Lighting* all written by Mike Lawrence and published by Crowood Press; these sister publications give step-by-step advice on techniques such as building studding walls and wiring in new lighting. Remember though that new building regulations, which do not usually apply to domestic refurbishments, are changing rapidly and you may be expected to show that work on some of these elements has been done by a 'competent' person.

Heating, lighting and decoration all have an important part to play in the finished bathroom. In terms of heating, that could be one of the 'designer' radiators that have come on the market over the past ten years or, even more recently, the use of under-floor heating for one of the non-carpet floor coverings that are so popular today. Lighting in bathrooms is moving toward support of the 'pampering' element of bathroom-use these days, with inset spot-lights and 'candle' effects being popular. Wall and floor tiling, or cladding with stones such as granite and marble, are also popular in the more luxurious bathrooms. In the UK we still tend to see decoration as a job to do once everything else is finished and we only apply decoration to the surfaces left exposed.

Some people, though, are beginning to follow the Continental practice of seeing floor and wall tiling as a part of the job that follows preparation and repositioning of services, and cover the whole floor with, say, ceramic tiling, and cover all wall surfaces with wall tiling or marble cladding; thus giving a seal to the whole room before installation of sanitaryware,

---

Guides to Good Installation

Ensure that your installation is in accordance with water regulations/bye-laws and with BS6700, which is the specification for design, installation, testing and maintenance of services supplying water for domestic use within buildings and their cartilages. The manufacturer's guidance on plumbing requirements must be followed.

---

baths and showering. In the UK we still have to be wary of this because some baths and shower-trays rely on an 'overlap' from the wall tiling to seal against water ingress to the fabric of the house.

In all of this preparatory work it is important to retain safe and hygienic facilities for the house.

Ventilation

Adequate ventilation, using an extractor fan, will keep mirrors and tiled surface free of condensation and reduce the growth of mould. There are several types of fan specifically designed for positioning above the bath or shower, and for wall, window or ceiling mounting. Extractor fans can be switched independently or via the light switch. Some have a humidistat, which automatically activates the extractor when the humidity reaches a certain level.

Ventilation – Building Regulations

The building regulations stipulate that mechanical ventilation must be installed in bath/shower rooms and toilets. Commercially available fans will comply with or exceed current building regulations and are capable of extracting not less than 15ltr/s from bath/shower rooms.

Specific requirements of *The Building Regulations Document F1* (1995 edition) on ventilation are as follows:
- bathrooms: the regulations require a fan capable of minimum extract capacity of 15ltr/s 54m³h (32CFM);
- toilets: the regulations require a fan capable of at least three air changes per hour and with a 15min over-run timer. (NB 15min over-run is not a requirement in Scotland.)

This modern bathroom uses candles to pamper the senses with warmth and gentle lighting. (Ideal Standard)

Pink marble cladding the walls and the countertop that takes the bath, with solid wooden flooring. (Mark Wilkinson)

It is recommended that the air in a bathroom is changed three times per hour, so to calculate what size of fan you need, measure the height, depth and width of the room – in metres – (typically 1.8 × 2 × 2.4m, which gives 8.6m³) then multiply the result (8.6) by the number of times per hour you need to change the air; for our typically small bathroom, an extractor that can clear over 26m³/h is ideal. The building regulations ask for over twice that capacity. Extractor fans can be fitted easily by the experienced DIY person, however, all electrical connections should be undertaken by a qualified electrician.

Let the fan continue to run for several minutes after taking a shower or a bath.

Understanding the Physics of Waste Removal

This short précis on the physics at work in a bathroom is not intended as an authoritative guide, merely to flag-up an aspect of bathroom design and installation that is rarely considered at the domestic refurbishment level – indeed, it very rarely applies due to the restricted size of UK bathrooms.

As you may be aware, the physics of the bathroom relies totally on gravity in its work as a practical removal mechanism for waste matter and used water. Internal waste-water pipes rely on sufficient gradient to clear the flow into the drains and give a velocity of water that will clean out the other detritus that goes down waste internal waste pipes.*

There is a whole-house consideration that relies on flow of water and on the venting of soil and water stacks to ensure that no air-locks disturb this flow. Also that no flow of water is so extreme that it creates a vacuum that sucks out the contents of the water-traps and allows sewage gases back into the house.

*Gradient is defined as between 18mm/m and 90mm/m. It is possible to drain bathroom and toilet waste 'uphill' using a pumping device known as a macerator.

It is not such a delicate balance that it should cause concern, but it is nonetheless a balance that you may disturb in some installations. Probably the area of bathroom installation where you are most likely to enter this world of physics is when fitting a shower-tray, especially with the growing fashion to have them as close to a level-entry as possible – at all times an adequate slope for the waste water pipe needs to be maintained.

Another consideration to bear in mind is the distance between the 'plug-hole' and the place where the waste pipe enters the main soil pipe or waste and vent pipe. For the modern single-stack systems it is advised that the basin is within 1.7m of the stack, as this appliance is considered to have the

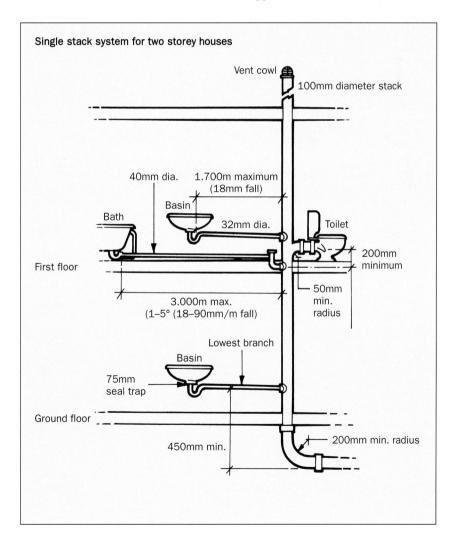

Be aware of the physics of waste removal but, other than the basin, this will normally only apply to larger bathrooms.

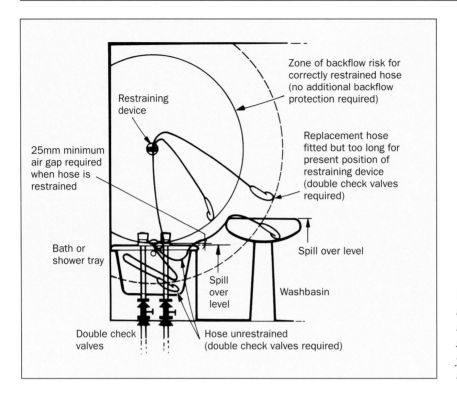

Zone of backflow risk for correctly restrained hose (no additional backflow protection required)

Restraining device

Replacement hose fitted but too long for present position of restraining device (double check valves required)

25mm minimum air gap required when hose is restrained

Bath or shower tray

Spill over level

Spill over level

Washbasin

Double check valves

Hose unrestrained (double check valves required)

Use a restraining device to stop used water from the bath or basin syphoning back into your water supply via the shower.

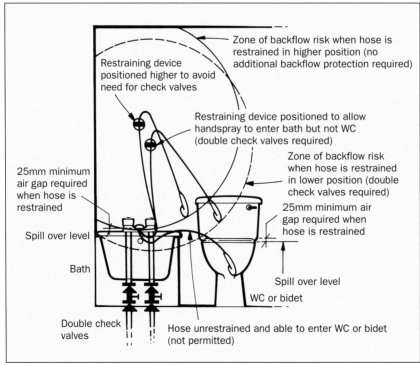

Zone of backflow risk when hose is restrained in higher position (no additional backflow protection required)

Restraining device positioned higher to avoid need for check valves

Restraining device positioned to allow handspray to enter bath but not WC (double check valves required)

Zone of backflow risk when hose is restrained in lower position (double check valves required)

25mm minimum air gap required when hose is restrained

25mm minimum air gap required when hose is restrained

Spill over level

Bath

Spill over level

WC or bidet

Double check valves

Hose unrestrained and able to enter WC or bidet (not permitted)

Water in a bidet or WC is a category five risk, which means that it represents a serious health hazard if it finds its way back into the water supply and as such it is better to fit a fixed shower-head rather than a flexible shower-head that risks being able to reach a source of serious contamination.

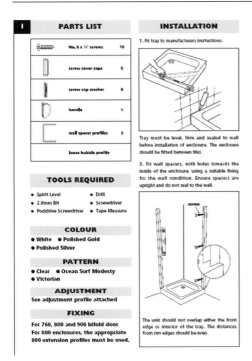

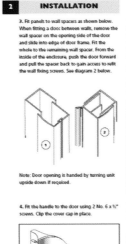

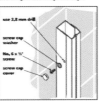

A good example of professionally presented installation instructions. (Trevi Showers)

highest risk of self-siphoning. This does also depend on the diameter of waste pipe used and 1.7m refers to a typical 32mm pipe being used. If a large 40mm-diameter pipe is used, then the building regulations allow for a 3m run of pipework from the basin to the stack. The pipe-run for a WC, which uses a much greater diameter of pipework, is: 'no more than 6m'.

BACK-SIPHONING OR BACK-FLOW

This is syphonic action – either inside a piece of brassware or a shower-hose – causing the air-gap to be bridged between the clean mains water, either in the mains supply or after it has been stored, and used (grey) water from the shower-tray, toilet bowl, bidet or even the bath. The grey water may be carrying bacteria or material that will encourage the growth of bacteria and contaminate the clean water supply to the house, or even to the neighbourhood. The danger of back-siphoning is that bacteria built up in used water may be introduced to drinking water. If left uncontrolled it could bring back diseases such as typhoid and cholera. A guide to Water Supply (water fittings) Regulations 1999

and the Water Bylaws 2000, Scotland is published by WRAS (Water Regulations Advisory Scheme) Fern Close, Pen-Y-Fan Industrial Estate, Oakdale, Newport, NP113EH. ISBN 0-9539708-0-9.

The water regulations require the installer to determine the level of back-flow prevention required for a particular installation. Water in a bath, shower-tray or washbasin is classified as a category three risk, which means that it represents a slight health hazard if it finds its way back into the water supply. To counter this health hazard it must not be possible for any flexible shower hose/shower-head to enter any adjacent bath, shower-tray or wash basin. If you want to use a flexible shower while in the bath, or while standing at the basin, then double-check valves must be fitted to both the hot supply and the cold supply to the bath/shower mixer – otherwise an air gap of at least 25mm must be maintained to avoid back-siphoning.

FITTING INSTRUCTIONS – READ THEM!

Most bathroom products come with very clear fitting instructions, but many fitting instructions do not get read until something has gone wrong. This heading

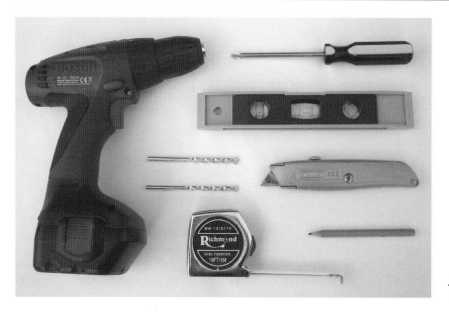

Tools will be those found in a typical home tool-kit.

may sound facetious but it is probably the most important in the book.

The fitting instructions are also a good guide to a good installer. The better installers will take the time to familiarize themselves with installation directions – even if they have fitted hundreds of bathrooms before, something may have changed. It also says something about the quality of the supplier, if they take the trouble to supply professionally presented fitting instructions.

TOOLS AND EQUIPMENT

The tools you will need to install the elements of the bathroom that we are covering here are found in most home tool-kits.

In most cases you need a spirit-level, electric drill with a range of drill-bits, tape-measure and screwdriver, as well, of course, as a pencil to mark out with and a Stanley knife. You will also need a selection of adjustable wrenches plus a set of open spanners, including a claw spanner for taps and a good method for applying sealants. In some cases, when fitting bath panels, there may be a need to cut them to size to suit the finished height, so there may be a need for a fine saw. If there is furniture to be fitted, a jigsaw may also be required.

One set of 'tools' you may not have considered is a pair of knee-pads. A large number of professional plumbers suffer from stressed knee-joints later in life, much the same way as footballers do. Readers, of course, will not be spending a lifetime on their knees, but neither will kneeling for an hour or two be something that you are used to; so, for the low costs involved, a set of knee-pads is a worthwhile investment.

Once the ripping-out and repositioning of service has been completed, fitting a bathroom should be a clean process, but a set of dust covers and masking equipment to protect any pre-finished surfaces are always appreciated by other members of the household – as is cleaning equipment to remove any dust created.

SAFETY

Most of us are getting used to doing safety-surveys these days, and before you start the project you do need to take a careful view of what you are capable of and what may go wrong. You probably will not be touching any of the lethal energies, like electricity or gas, and you are unlikely to be allowed to do so by law. However, when it comes to water, you may well be working with one of the most damaging and invasive of substances. Therefore, you must not stray into an area where the work causes damage that your insurance provider will refuse to cover because it was not completed by a competent person.

CHAPTER 4

Baths

Bathing in the home began in the late-Victorian era. For wealthier families, the bath was made from fire-clay or enamelled cast-iron, while working-class families either used public baths or had a galvanized-tin bath that they brought it into the house once a week to take their bath in the living room, usually just in front of the fire. Enamelled steel followed in the twentieth century and still has a use in heavy-wear markets such as hotels, hospitals, student accommodation and some social housing.

Today, reinforced acrylic is the material that has virtually taken over as the material from which we make 90 per cent of baths. The more luxurious cast-iron models, meanwhile, have been replaced by a much lighter and temperature-friendly cast-resin material, which is used by modern designers to create the neo-Victorian roll-top baths and the more contemporary designer baths. Technology too has entered the more luxurious end of the bath market with a variety of whirlpool and spa baths, again mainly produced from acrylic or cast-resin.

MATERIALS AND CONSTRUCTION METHODS

Vacuum-Formed Acrylic Baths Reinforced With Fibreglass

The acrylic used to make baths is a material that was once better known by brand names such as Perspex. The name has changed, for the bathroom, but the basic material is the same. An acrylic bath starts life as a flat sheet, which is warmed up in a warming-oven until it is pliable. The sheet is then lifted on to a jig, where it is clamped in place over a metal former that

will give it its final shape. Air is first pumped into the former and then pumped out to form the vacuum that sucks the acrylic sheet into shape. At this stage, the bath is very light and the overall shape will easily flex. To give the acrylic shape its strength, the bath then has a chipboard baseboard positioned underneath, and the underside of the bath is covered in a generous strengthening of fibreglass.

Some models have the baseboard completely encapsulated in strengthening, while others are left uncovered. The cost and the price often vary, depending upon how thoroughly the acrylic is strengthened, as well as the complexity of the shape. The acrylic bath then has a wooden or a metal strengthening frame fixed underneath the outside rim, and a metal cradle (sometimes with adjustable legs) is provided to ensure that the bath can easily be installed at an accurate level.

The baths are manufactured from a range of acrylic sheets having different thicknesses, typically 4mm, 5mm or 8mm. As a rule, the greater the thickness, the less GRP reinforcement is needed on the underside.

Porcelain-Enamel Steel Baths

Steel baths are formed on a metal-press from a thin steel sheet to give them their shape. After pressing, the bath is covered on its interior face with porcelain

---

Did You Know...?

90 per cent of baths are made from acrylic sheet - it is a superb material.

Making an acrylic bath. Top to bottom: acrylic sheet being moulded to the shape of a bath; at this stage it is very light and the shape will flex; fibreglass strengthening is applied to the base of a bath by a spray gun; the finished bath is cleaned-up prior to packing. (Jacuzzi)

enamel, which is a form of glass bonded to the metal at high temperature. The vitreous porcelain-enamel coat is applied by spraying. The baths are then fired at a very high temperature to make a strong chemical bond between the steel and the enamel. Porcelain-enamel steel baths have inherent strength and generally do not need an under-rim supporting frame or a baseboard. They are supplied with adjustable feet to allow levelling on uneven floors and some adjustment of the installation height.

Cast-Iron Baths

Cast-iron baths are no longer manufactured by the mainstream bath producers in the UK, which makes them quite rare. In spite of this they remain a favourite with some interior designers.

Cast-iron baths are made by pouring molten iron into a mould. After forming, they are subject to a cleaning process to ensure that the surface of the iron bonds with the porcelain enamel sprayed on to their surface. Baths then undergo treatment at high temperatures in a kiln to bond the coating to the surface. Cast-iron baths are very strong and need no other form of strengthening. They are free-standing and are carried on support-feet, which are bolted on to each corner.

These baths are very heavy, and the level and strength of the supporting floor is of paramount importance. It is very unusual to seal a cast-iron bath to the wall. In reality, cast-resins have all but taken over from cast-iron baths.

Cast-Resin Baths

Cast-resin is the modern material that is used when the design of a bath requires great strength; it is prevalent in the modern free-standing baths and to replicate old styles that were originally made from cast-iron or fireclay. So, some of the larger modern baths, particularly the two-person baths, are made from cast-resin, as are shower-baths, which require a strong base for the user to stand on. For these baths the inner facing of the bath is produced from vacuum-formed acrylic, as described previously. This inner facing is then placed in a mould and the resin is

OPPOSITE: Double-ended steel bath. (Kaldewei)

This Victorian-style, roll-top bath made from cast-resin, is modelled after the cast-iron original. (BMA)

poured in. When set, the resin gives the bath its rigidity and strength. This method was initially used to form replicas of the old cast-iron roll-top baths, but more and more these days cast-resin is being used for modern, free-standing and designer-shape baths.

The latest baths use a number of different support systems; popular features include wooden feet or cradles, or metal cradles.

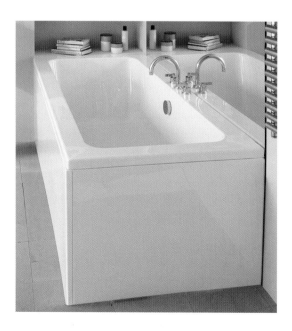

An acrylic bath. (Ideal Standard)

CHARACTERISTICS

Each of the four materials – vacuum-formed reinforced acrylic; porcelain-enamelled pressed-steel; enamelled cast-iron or cast-resin – have particular characteristics, which influence the design and application of the baths that they form. For example, vacuum-formed acrylic is easily moulded into a wide variety of shapes and styles. It is an economically priced material, all of which contributes to that fact that acrylic baths are the most popular choice for British bathrooms. Around 90 per cent of all baths bought for bathroom refurbishment, or fitted into new houses, are produced from acrylic sheet. The 'standard' rectangular shape that is 1,700 × 700mm in size has become so strongly accepted that most houses built in the past 25 years have bathrooms built to suit this sizing.

Acrylic

Vacuum-formed acrylics have characteristics such as:

- retaining water temperature longer than baths made from metal;
- lightweight;
- easily transported;
- easy to install;
- easy to keep clean;
- strong and hard-wearing;
- excellent resistance to water staining;
- small scratches can be polished out;
- available in a wide range of colours (although the current fashion is for white);
- available in a wide range of shapes, sizes and tap-positions;
- reasonably priced.

Steel

Porcelain-enamel steel baths have characteristics such as:

- smooth and evenly finished;
- easy to install, generally having no need of an under-rim support cradle;
- good rigidity;
- resistant to acids and alkalis;

Corner bath in enamelled steel. (Kaldewei)

- capable of supporting heavier weights;
- long-lasting (flame-proof, fade-proof, corrosion-resistant);
- the surface can chip (not easily) and, if that happens, the enamel is difficult to repair;
- like all metal baths, steel can be something of a heat-sink in colder installations;
- enamelled steel is hard-wearing and its robust nature makes it a favourite for social housing and hotels.

Cast-Iron

Cast-iron has similar properties to steel baths:

- immensely strong and solid;
- very rigid;
- coated with porcelain enamel for easy cleaning;
- associated with traditional bathrooms;
- durable with a long life;
- easy to clean.

Drawbacks of cast-iron are its weight and the way that the metal will draw the heat out of the bathwater in colder installations. Cast-iron baths also tend to be more expensive, very heavy and need great care in handling during installation.

Cast-Resin

Cast-resin has a mixture of the properties of acrylic and cast-iron baths, such as:

- immensely strong and solid;
- very rigid;
- coated with acrylic for easy cleaning;

- durable with a long life;
- warm.

Drawbacks of cast-resin are that it is a more complex manufacturing process and, therefore, more expensive than acrylic baths.

SHAPES OR TYPES AND SIZES AVAILABLE

Baths made from both acrylic and steel come in a range of shapes and sizes.

Standard Bath

Rectangular in shape and with numerous size options, standard baths can be supplied with front and end panels. These panels are usually made from plastics and are lightweight and easy to cut to fit into various installation situations. Whilst 1,700 × 700mm is the most common size, it is possible to obtain a wide range of other sizes. Some manufacturers make acrylic and steel baths with double-curved ends. The bath-panels are usually supplied in plastics to finish the front and ends. Some specialist manufacturers provide highly decorated steel bath-panels.

Corner Baths

These baths fit into a corner of the bathroom, usually with each side being of equal lengths. Front panels are usually made from plastics and they come in a variety of designs, which, like the standard bath, are easily cut and trimmed to fit specific installations/conditions.

Off-Set Corner Baths

These baths fit into a corner of the bathroom but have sides of unequal length. This optimizes bathing space, whilst occupying less of the available space. Off-set corner baths fit into left- or right-hand corners of the bathroom, as required. They are available in a range of styles and colours.

Shower-Baths

Shower-baths provide conventional bathing with the additional facility of an over-the-bath shower. The showering end of the bath generally displays a 'bulge' or widening to maximize space for showering. These baths are available in left- or right-handed options to fit into most bathroom layouts.

Tapered Baths

Tapered baths are designed to be used in bathrooms where space is at a premium. These baths are wider at one end. Often a shower is fitted at the wider end.

They are available in a range of colours and sizes. These baths are supplied with matching side-panels.

Twin Baths

These baths are usually rectangular in shape with a facility for fitting the taps on one of the sides rather than at either end. This allows two people to bathe together or for a number of children to be bathed at the same time. Bathing with a partner is no longer considered even risqué and most manufacturers' ranges have baths that suit two people, these tend to be produced in the stronger materials like steel and cast-resin.

Cast-Iron Baths

These baths are generally free-standing with decorative feet, sometimes called 'claw feet'. Styles tend to be anything but 'standard', with representations of early-Victorian slipper baths to late-Victorian and Edwardian free-standing roll-top baths.

Shower-bath with standing area at the tap-end of the bath. (Ideal Standard)

Twin-ended bath. (Kaldewei)

Shower-bath in cast-resin, modelled after a Victorian original that would have been produced in cast-iron. (Ideal Standard)

Cast-Resin Baths

Standard Baths

Not many standard 1,700 × 700mm baths are made from cast-resin. If they are they tend to have much thinner sides and rims, which is due to the inherent strength of the material.

Free-Standing Baths

Cast-resin is ideal for free-standing baths. From Victorian reproductions through to the very latest fashions, this material is often supplied with the outside un-coloured, so that it can be painted to suit the decor of the room. The one drawback is price.

Shower-baths

Shower-baths are a great solution for the smaller bathroom, which otherwise would not have room for a shower. Shower-baths have a widened area at the tap-end of the bath, with a flat floor to the showering end, which makes standing much easier.

SPECIFYING THE CORRECT BATH FOR YOUR NEEDS

Children
It is important to think about the bath that will best match your life-style. If you have a young family, a twin-ended bath helps at busy times. (Kaldewei)

Inclusive
If you have family members suffering from age-related conditions, such as arthritis that make them unsteady on their feet, then a transfer shelf at the end of the bath will help them get in and out, while providing towel access for fitter family members. (Kaldewei)

GUIDE TO INSTALLING BATHS

Whichever shape or material of bath that you choose there are three 'basics' to keep in mind for a successful installation:

1. You will need to ensure that the top rim of the bath is level along its length and width, so careful use of the spirit-level is key.
2. You will need to know that the bath is well sealed along any edges that butt-up to the wall. Wall coverings, such as ceramic tiles or marble, can be fixed to overlap the rim to help the final sealant to do its work.
3. Finally, spend time to ensure that the hidden connections to taps and waste pipes are soundly fixed and waterproof.

Another major consideration when fitting a larger, perhaps two-person, bath is to ensure that the house has a large enough supply of water to cope with a single filling.

Essentially, the methods of installing baths are the same no matter what materials are used in their manufacture but there are variations that must be considered. The tools needed to fit a bath are, in the main, a spirit-level and adjustable wrench, screwdriver and an electric drill. Some baths are supplied without tap-holes to give a choice of fixing – for these you would need a hole-drill.

Acrylic

Before fixing a new acrylic bath or its panels, remove the clear protective covering and check thoroughly that all the components required have been supplied by the manufacturer. Manufacturers' instructions will vary for different models and between different manufacturers, so always read the specific instructions carefully before commencing work.

Acrylic baths are supplied with a metal support cradle, which is fitted out of sight underneath the bath. The cradle has adjustable feet that allow the bath to be levelled on uneven floors during installation. The cradle is usually packed with the bath and requires assembling prior to installation. Some acrylic baths come with the cradle ready assembled, but in most cases you will need to fix this in place. It seems obvious to say that this is foundation work and must not be left off, yet one of the most common installation faults reported to manufacturers is baths that have simply been placed on the floor without their support cradle fitted. To allow for the water to drain

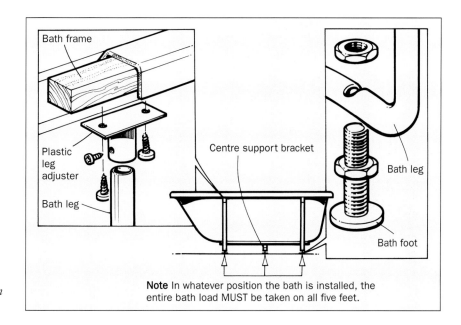

Example of the instructions for fitting the support mechanism to an acrylic bath.

Bath frame

Plastic leg adjuster

Bath leg

Centre support bracket

Bath leg

Bath foot

Note In whatever position the bath is installed, the entire bath load MUST be taken on all five feet.

fully out of the bath, the base is not necessarily level and any bath fitted this way will invariably drain badly. The easiest way to fit the metal cradle to the underside of the bath is to invert the bath, but put a cloth sheet on the floor first so as not to scratch the surface of the bath.

Being careful to follow the manufacturer's instructions, especially on such things as drill depths and screw-fixing depths, fit the cradle legs to the frame and baseboard, and also fit the centre support leg, if one is supplied. While the bath is inverted, fix the waste fittings and set the adjustment on the feet to suit the height shown in the fitting instructions.

Some baths are supplied with a choice of tap positions, so there may be a need to drill holes for the taps – instructions for doing this may be included with the bath, or they may be included with the taps. With taps that require two or more tap-holes, look for a positioning template.

Attach the wall-fixing brackets (if supplied) to the underside of the rim-support frame. Fit any hand grip(s) to the rim, if supplied, at this point so that you have easy access to the securing nuts and washers. When wall fixing brackets are supplied by the manufacturer, it is important that they are used and it is often easier to fit them to the bath while it is inverted; it is considered good practice to drill pilot holes into the bath frame before fixing brackets. The purpose of the wall-fixing brackets is to prevent movement or 'play' at the point where the bath meets the wall.

At this point, turn the bath back on to its feet. Initially, place the bath in the required position to adjust the bath to the height shown in the fixing instructions, by using the adjustable feet. When you are satisfied that the overall height is correct, ensure that the bath is level by using a spirit-level across the width and the length of the bath. 'Fine tune' to the correct level and tighten the locking nuts on all of the feet. Pull the bath away from the wall and install the other components.

Place the hot and cold taps, or a mixer-tap set, through the pre-cut holes on the bath rim, ensuring the rubber/plastic washers are located under the body of the taps against the bath. Attach and tighten the locking nuts from the underside. Attach flexible connecting pipes to the tap tails – this allows for any

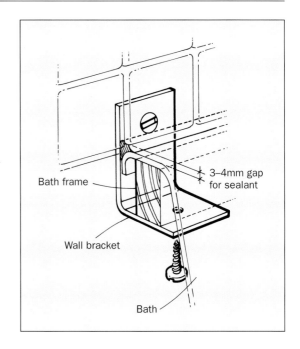

Fixing the bath to the wall using fixing brackets screwed into the timber frame – positioned to leave a gap for sealant.

misalignment when you connect the taps to the water-supply pipes.

Complete fitting the overflow outlet and waste outlet to the bath, again ensuring that all the necessary washers are located in their correct position. Connect them to the combined waste/overflow and trap unit. When all of the components have been correctly fitted, place the bath back in its desired position, re-check the levels and secure to the wall with the brackets. Connect the water-supply and waste-pipes. Before completing the installation it is recommended that the bath is fully filled with warm water to allow it to 'settle' on the frame and fittings, as acrylic material tends to flex slightly.

In the UK, the general practice is that tiling is completed after the bath has been fixed to the wall so that the tiles overlap on to the bath rim with a 3–4mm-gap. This leaves a joint between the wall and bath that can be filled using a proprietary waterproof flexible silicone sealant. So that this seal can be made more easily watertight, do this work while the bath is still full of water. Any movement of the bath relative to the wall can lead to leakage, particularly if a shower is used over the bath.

For many years, the practice in most European countries has been to tile the whole bathroom prior to installation, to create a fully sealed room, walls and floor; this has not been an option for the UK, where cosiness in our cooler bathrooms was supplied by carpets. However, with the growth in under-floor heating, this practice is beginning to change and some of us may decide to adopt the Continental attitude to tiling.

With the bath fixed into position, the last thing to fit is the bath panel. Begin by 'test fitting' the bath panel(s) to the bath to see how much (if any) they will need trimming to ensure a neat and tidy finish. Panels are commonly supplied slightly larger than required, so that they can be trimmed to individual installation requirements. Always use a fine-toothed saw, being careful not to scratch the surface of the panel. Individual manufacturer's panels are fitted in different ways, so read their specific installation instructions carefully.

Steel Bath Installation

Installation of a steel bath follows the same principles as for acrylic baths but there are a few differences. Normally, because a steel bath is inherently more rigid than an acrylic bath, it is supported by a cradle fixed directly to the base of the bath, rather than one that supports the whole of the bath. All the same fixing instructions apply, except that it is not necessary to fill the bath prior to sealing, as the steel bath will not deform when filled. Bear in mind that a steel bath will probably be heavier than its acrylic equivalent and may need two people to handle safely.

Cast-Iron Bath Installation

Installation of a cast-iron bath will definitely need two strong and fit people to manoeuvre into position. The strength and the level of the floor will be paramount to the success of the installation. The floor will need to be completely finished before installation, as there will be no bath-panels. The floor finish needs to be able to cope with the four points of loading – the feet. Ceramic tiles may not be suitable,

as they may crack if the loading is too great or the floor has some flex in it.

A cast-iron bath is supported by the feet, which are an integral part of the casting or are attached separately. There is no additional cradle for support, as a cast-iron bath is completely rigid and self-supporting. Because there is no cradle that needs to be hidden, cast-iron baths are typically of 'free-standing' design in a luxury-style bathroom, in that they are not attached to any walls.

Cast-Resin Bath Installation

All but the very large cast-resin baths are usually light enough to handle, and the same fixing techniques as an acrylic bath will apply. The exceptions being that there are usually no bath panels and often the outer finish is intended to be painted – after installation. Also it is more likely that the bath will not be drilled for tap-holes. Indeed some cast-resin baths have taps that are wall-fixed or are fixed on a tap-tower that is fixed to the floor.

SAFETY AND HEALTH

Handling

Safety considerations when installing a bath mainly revolve around handling the heavier and larger baths, and in these cases common sense applies – trying to handle a cast-iron, or even cast-resin, bath without enough people or the correct equipment is not safe.

Safety When Stepping Into and Out of a Bath

There are also safety considerations when planning the bathroom in which the bath sits. For older people, the bath can be quite daunting and many have fears of falling while getting into and out of the bath. The use of plastic mats, with suckers on the underside, also illustrates a more general concern about stepping into and out of the bath or standing in a bath to use the shower. Manufacturers' opinions vary as to whether a completely flat surface to the base of the bath is the safest option (such that the whole imprint of the foot meets the surface) or whether a series of indents should be shaped into the base of the bath to allow the water to run away more easily and remove the soapy water, which is seen as the primary cause of slipping. Either is an acceptable finish for a domestic bath and sensible use, with care, renders the concern unviable. Some of the metal baths used in hotels have a 'sand-paper-like' finish to reduce the chance of slipping, although this finish is not necessarily nice to look at.

For older people, who may be unsteady on their feet, a method for entering and leaving a bath that is recommended by occupational therapists, is to build a platform at the end of the bath for the user to sit on. By swinging their feet around into the bath it is then easy and very safe to slide down into the bath. Getting out of the bath is a reverse of this process with the bather first kneeling to face the platform, then standing, turning and sitting on the platform and then swinging their legs out of the bath and on to the floor. This is also a method that can be used by wheelchair users.

Whirlpool jet in operation. (Jacuzzi)

These fears can be allayed by using aids, such as hand grips (although care is still needed, since older people may not have a very strong grip in their hands) and specialist equipment, such as bath hoists and seats.

Use

Allowing young children to use the bath unsupervised cannot be recommended. Another current topic of concern is that of scalding from baths filled with water above the mid-forty degrees temperature. Currently the regulation bodies and bath manufacturers are working on thermostatic bath-fillers and basin-fillers to reduce this potential danger.

Fire

While slipping and falling are the major safety concern, users of acrylic baths are advised by the fire service to be careful if they surround the rim of the bath with candles. There have been cases of candles being left and allowed to burn down and setting fire to the acrylic of the bath.

WHIRLPOOL BATHS

'Whirlpool' is a general term for the two different methods of activating water in a bath:

- **Whirlpool bath.** Typically, in this type of bath, jets are set into the inner surface of the bath. The water from the bath is drawn into a pump and returned through the jets at high pressure. The stop/start, mixture of air and water and flow rate are adjusted by a control panel, which is either located on the rim of the bath or may be a remote-control, similar to a television.
- **Spa bath.** The spa bath uses air, where the whirlpool uses water – a pump forces the air upwards through the bath water via jets located in the inner surface of the bath; again the flow rate is governed by a control panel.

Whirlpool/spa baths are available in numerous shapes and styles and are mostly manufactured in acrylic. As with 'standard' baths they are supported by a cradle, which also acts as a convenient location for the pump and associated pipework.

A combined term for whirlpool and spa baths, and some super-showers, is 'wellness'. (Kaldewei)

A control panel mounted on the rim of the bath. (Bronte)

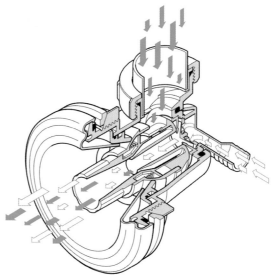

Cut-out showing the mixture of water and air. (Jacuzzi)

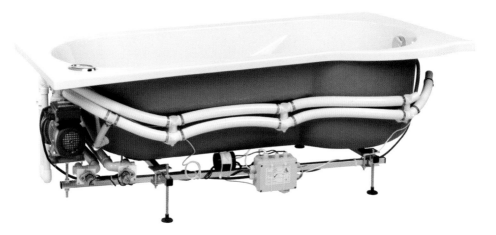

It is important to allow access to the services after installation is complete. (Bronte)

Whirlpool Bath Installation

Because of their more complex nature, whirlpool baths must be installed by qualified plumbers and electricians.

A few general tips would include:

- avoid carrying or lifting the bath using any part of the pipework;
- always allow access to service the whirlpool or spa after installation, and install the bath in such a manner that will allow for its removal without the necessity to remove fixed wall-tiles;
- when you unpack the bath, check that the pump unions are hand-tight only and that nothing has been moved in transit;
- fit stop-valves in to the water supply to allow the water to be turned off when necessary;
- inspect the bath for damage before installation;
- never run the whirlpool system without water in the bath, as this can damage the pump.

Electrical Requirements

The electrical installation *must* be carried out by a qualified electrician. Note the following:

- mains supply via a 30MA, 30ms RCD (residual current device);
- use a 13A-fused spur from the ring main;
- use 2.5 twin and earth cable.

RCD (Residual Current Device)

- The RCD must not be fitted under the bath.
- The RCD must not be fitted within reach of the bath.
- The RCD must be positioned in an accessible position to allow for testing and can be used to isolate the bath.
- The bath and whirlpool pump must be correctly earthed.

Safety Issues

Safety is of paramount importance in the installation and use of whirlpool bath, as the combination of water and electricity is potentially a major hazard. Professional installation is a major priority to ensure that the highest safety standards are adhered to. Some baths are fitted with a safety cut-off unit in the event of the pump inlet becoming covered or with a safety suction cover. All whirlpool system should comply with EN60 335 Pt 2 safety standard.

Additional Information

There is a general recommendation that pregnant women and people with a medical condition should consult their doctor before taking a whirlpool bath or spa bath, and common sense would ensure that children, the very elderly or the infirm are not left unattended.

CHAPTER 5

Sanitaryware

Sanitaryware has become the generic term for the elements of the bathroom that are typically manufactured from vitreous china: the toilet bowl and cistern; the basin and pedestal, and also the bidet and urinal. Vitreous china is also known as ceramic and as pottery. These days sanitaryware is produced almost exclusively in a white glaze finish. Manufacturers believe sanitaryware to be the best material to cope with the functional demands of toileting and washing.

Other materials used in the manufacture of 'sanitary products' includes fireclay, acrylic and resin mixtures, glass, stainless steel and high-impact plastics, but these are relatively rare and this book will concentrate on the ceramic sanitaryware that readers are most likely to encounter.

A full set of sanitaryware – basin, pedestal. (BMA)

A full set of sanitaryware – WC and bidet. (BMA)

The main consideration, when choosing sanitary-ware, will lie in a balance between cost, style and performance. In addition, to ensure that the most suitable sanitaryware is selected, it is essential to consider the infrastructure and waste, and the water-supply system of the building in which the sanitary-ware is being installed.

MATERIALS AND CONSTRUCTION METHODS

Vitreous china is a very organic material, made from a mixture of china clay and ball clay, fluxes, water and a covering of glaze. There are a variety of modern methods of manufacture, most of which are developments of the old traditional methods for casting pottery. The traditional method, called bench-casting, involves a caster, who pours a finely sieved mixture of 'water, clays and minerals', called 'slip', into plaster moulds, which form the shape of the piece being cast. The surplus water from the 'slip' is absorbed by the plaster over a period of hours.

Although more simple shapes can be moulded in one piece, the more intricate shapes, with ornate detailing on the exterior and complex water channels

Factors Affecting the Price

The different methods of casting require different mould structures and different production time and labour input, which is one of the factors that sees a wide variance in the cost of seemingly similar products.

within the body of the piece – such as is found in toilet pans – require multi-piece moulds and are still made in the traditional way.

More modern batch-casting (which still uses plaster moulds) and pressure-casting (which uses moulds made from resinous materials) bring a production-line technique to more simple or mass-produced shapes of sanitaryware. With pressure-casting it is the pressure applied that 'forces' the water out, rather than the plaster mould absorbing water from the liquid clay.

When the clay is dry enough to be self-supporting, it is in what is called its 'green' state and is removed from the mould. While still in its green state, final trimming or 'fettling' is carried out and any holes (such as tap-holes on the basins) are cut into the piece by hand.

1.

2.

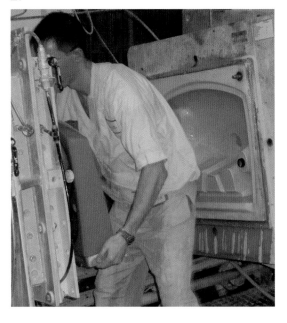

ABOVE: *Sanitaryware begins life as a flowing mixture of clays and water called slip. (Armitage Shanks)*

RIGHT: *The moulding being removed from a pressure-casting unit. (Armitage Shanks)*

3.

The moulding being fettled, while it is still in its 'green' state. (Armitage Shanks)

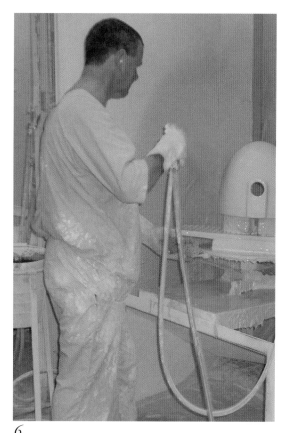

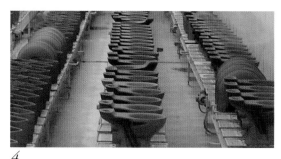

4.

The moulding has to be thoroughly dried prior to glazing – it starts in the atmosphere before moving into drying ovens. (Armitage Shanks)

6.

Glaze is sprayed on, either manually or by robot. (Armitage Shanks)

5.

Once dry the piece is said to be in its 'white' state and is ready for glazing prior to firing in the kiln. (Armitage Shanks)

7.

After glazing the piece spends 24h in a kiln being vitrified. (Armitage Shanks)

The piece is then thoroughly dried in gas-fired or microwave ovens – any water left in the piece would cause damage during firing. Most commonly this damage is seen as tiny pin holes (which are tiny blemishes) in the surface of the glaze. In fact, it is not unusual to find 'pin-holes' in the surface of a piece of pottery. If unsightly, these will be repaired during the manufacturing process by having the piece re-fired.

Once dry, the piece is in its 'white' stage and is then coated with a glaze, which can be any colour, but today is usually white. The clay pieces then move slowly through a kiln and are vitrified at a temperature of around 1,200°C. The whole process, from casting to final examination after firing, takes several days.

Expect Pin-Holes

It is not uncommon for pin-holes to be left in the surface, if they are not clearly visible, i.e. if you see a pin-hole on the underside of a basin during installation, that is to be expected. Pin-holes are a natural occurrence of pottery manufacture.

CHARACTERISTICS OF SANITARYWARE

Once installed, sanitaryware is very unlikely to wear out and can only be damaged under determined attack. Vitreous china items are best cleaned frequently using warm soapy water or mild detergent (a little disinfectant may be added). Rinse with clean water then dry with a soft cloth. Prompt and thorough cleaning immediately after use will prevent the build up of insoluble lime salts in hard-water areas and 'tide-mark' deposits. WC bowls should be cleaned regularly. Always clean under the rim. Flush after cleaning to remove any deposits of cleanser from the sump of the trap. Ensure that the frequency of flushing is in line with water regulations.

WATER-CLOSETS

Shapes or Types and Sizes Available
A modern water-closet is made up of three pieces of 'ware': the closet or pan that we sit on; the cistern

that carries the flushing-water and flushing-mechanism; and the cistern lid. There are six basic types of water-closet, which are described as: close-coupled; low-level; high-level; back-to-wall or concealed; wall-hung and squatting.

Close-Coupled
This type of WC is typically floor-mounted with the water-cistern resting on an extended platform at the back of the WC pan. The cistern is fixed directly to the WC using a washer to provide a water-tight seal. In other words, there is no visible pipe between the cistern and the pan.

Low-Level
The description 'low-level' refers to the height of the water cistern that carries the water to flush the pan. In the case of a low-level WC, the pan is floor-mounted with the cistern mounted separately on the wall. A short flush-pipe connects the cistern to the WC. When it comes to the height of the seat, the

Close-coupled WC, where the cistern sit on the pan. (BMA)

ABOVE: Low-level WC. (Armitage Shanks)

RIGHT: High-level WC. (Armitage Shanks)

most common height for any of the pan-type WCs is 400mm, but if you need a higher seat position, for taller people or for people with difficulty sitting or rising, there is a growing variety of heights and shapes being produced to suit individual needs.

High-Level

The pan is exactly the same as the low-level arrangement but the cistern is mounted high on the wall with a longer flush-pipe. This is more commonly used in commercial establishments, although some nostalgic styles are still arranged with high-level cisterns, usually with a polished brass delivery pipe connecting cistern to pan.

Back-to-Wall or Concealed

With a back-to-wall design, the pan still stands on the floor but the cistern is hidden behind a false wall with just the flushing mechanism showing. In this

---

High- and Low-Level Cistern Installation

It is important that the manufacturers' recommended dimensions are followed when determining the fixing height. If flush-pipes are shortened, the flush will be weakened and the pan contents may not be cleared effectively. For a low-level installation, the top of the cistern is usually set at 1,000mm above the floor. High-level installations usually have the underside of the cistern set at about 2,000mm from the floor; but in both cases, follow the manufacturers' recommendations.

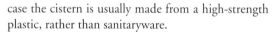

Back-to-wall WC. (BMA)

Wall-hung WC. (Jacuzzi)

case the cistern is usually made from a high-strength plastic, rather than sanitaryware.

At one time, back-to-wall was more commonly used in commercial applications (public toilets, etc.), where the lack of the exposed cistern aided cleaning, but there is now a trend to install this style in modern domestic installations.

Squatting pan. (BMA)

Wall-Hung
The WC pan is mounted on brackets fixed to the wall, which leaves an open floor space beneath the toilet. Once only seen on the Continent, the trend toward more simple interior-styling has seen the wall-hung pan grow in popularity in British homes.

Wall-hung is practical, in as much as it is ideal for easy floor cleaning and it gives a feeling of 'added' space in smaller bathrooms, although in reality the cistern has to be hidden behind a false wall that may reduce the floor area by 300mm or so. Many designers see the wall-hung toilet as the definition piece of a stylish bathroom.

Squatting
The WC pan is mounted at floor level, where the user 'straddles' the unit. In the UK, this design is more commonly associated with ethnic minorities, whose culture stems from countries such as India or China, although squat WCs can be found throughout Europe. In fact the public lavatories in the Vatican use squat toilets.

Mechanics and Fittings of a WC

WC Pan Waste Outlet Types
A water-barrier of 50mm is designed into the toilet pan – as it is in the other pieces of sanitaryware connected to the drains – the purpose of which is to prevent fumes and odours from the sewers escaping into the bathroom. Generally, the part of the sanitaryware or outlet pipe that contains these water barriers is described as a 'trap'.

The water-barrier is changed every time the toilet is flushed and the shape of the trap, plus the design of the plumbing system, ensures that a quantity of water is retained in the trap to ensure the barrier remains in place. The various shapes of the water-trap define what we call them.

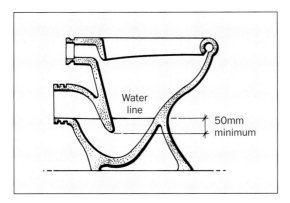

Water-trap of 50mm forms a barrier to prevent odours from the drains escaping into the house.

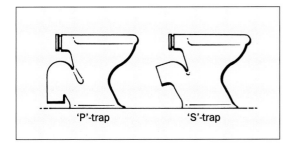

The old WCs had a 'P'-trap or an 'S'-trap cast into the pan.

In the past, WCs were manufactured with either a 'P'-trap or an 'S'-trap, which was included as an integral part of the casting, and you may come across these older models in a bathroom that is about to be refurbished. Today nearly all WC's have a simple horizontal outlet cast into the pan and the trap is an external device with connection to the drains made by plastic connectors that are available in a number on configurations that replicate the 'P' and 'S' configurations.

WC Flushing Operation
In terms of clearing the pan of all waste, there are two main types of flushing mechanisms, known as washdown and syphonic.

Washdown In this type, the pan is cleared by careful distribution of the force and volume of the flush water. Washdown pans retain a 50mm water-seal and a convenient bowl shaped to provide efficient cleaning and to minimize fouling. This type is by far the most common type of WC installed in the UK.

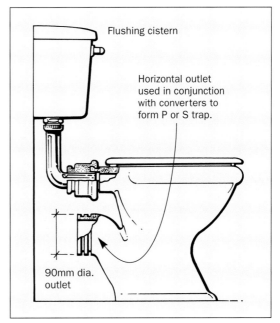

A modern washdown pan with horizontal outlet and a low-level cistern.

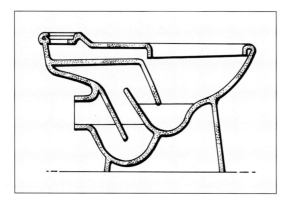

Old-style syphonic pan.

Syphonic The syphonic pan is becoming a thing of the past due to the 2001 changes in regulations that have restricted the flushing volumes. You may come across a syphonic pan if you are working on an existing installation. Basically, with this type of pan, the flow of water in the flushing operation creates suction that assists the clearance of solids from the pan. A double-trap syphonic WC is very quiet and efficient in operation; it has an unrestricted full-bore trap arrangement that reduces the risk of blockage and needs the higher flush volumes to work effectively.

Fixing WC Pans

It is essential that WC pans are solidly fixed so that they can safely carry people of all weights and sizes. They must be fixed to a level floor by screws using the pre-cast holes provided – this applies whether on wooden or concrete floors.

Some closets have a special floor bracket and are fixed to the bracket, which give them their purchase to the floor. No matter which fixing method applies, brass screws should be used to prevent rusting and

---

Changes in Regulations

Recent changes in legislation now allow a low-level WC suite with close-coupled pan to be fitted with a bottom outlet without having to move the soil pipe.

---

care should be taken to align them with the angle of the fixing holes.

Silicone is the material normally used to seal the bottom of the WC pan to the floor. Alternatively, this joint between the pan and floor can be 'pointed' with a cement mortar for decorative effect but on no account should WC pans rely on its floor fixing by being set on to a solid bed of concrete or the foot of the pan may split.

Plastic connectors should be used to connect the horizontal outlet to the soil-pipe that carries the waste from the house and into the sewers. Many different designs of plastic connectors are available to suit all installations.

Water-Closet Cisterns

The cistern is the part of the toilet that stores the water to be used for flushing and contains the mechanism that controls the flush. On the close-coupled and low-level flushing toilets, the body of the cistern is usually produced from vitreous china, to match the pan. These WC cistern bodies consist of two parts: the water sump, which is the greater part, and the lid.

Water is piped into the cistern from the bottom of the cistern (bottom-inlet) or from the side of the cistern (side-inlet) and redirected into the pan via the flushing system.

In manufacture, all sanitaryware shrinks during its passage through the kiln and, while the sump and the lid are 'cast' separately to ensure the best possible fit, they are put together before firing so that they follow a similar process of shrinkage in the extreme heat of the kiln. Readers should not expect such a good 'fit' if the original lid becomes damaged and has to be replaced.

Fixing the WC Cistern

The final stage of fixing the complete WC is to offer the cistern to the wall and mark for screw holes. At this point, on a modern, close-coupled WC, the cistern must sit square on to the pan. It is bad practice to use the wall screws to draw the cistern back to the wall – such a practice strains the seal between cistern and pan, and will lead to seepage and possible breakage.

Heavy duty plastic is the alternative material that may be used to manufacture a high-level cistern.

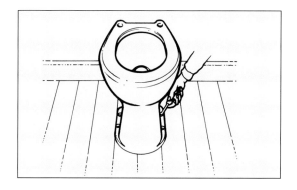

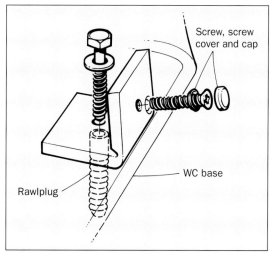

Screw, screw
cover and cap

Rawlplug

WC base

ABOVE: Where the pan is fixed directly to the floor, stand the bowl in the correct position and mark the position of screw holes, then move the pan to drill pilot holes for the rawlplugs.

ABOVE RIGHT: Here metal brackets are screwed into the floor. The base, or foot, of the WC bowl is then screwed into the bracket.

RIGHT: Pan fixed to brackets. An example of fixing method carried in manufacturers' instructions: stand the bowl in position; draw around the base; mark the bracket positions as shown in instructions.

BELOW: Plastic connectors to fix WC pan to the soil pipe come in a number of configurations.

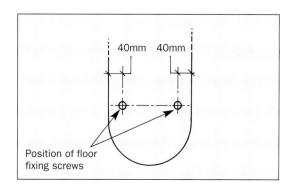

40mm   40mm

Position of floor
fixing screws

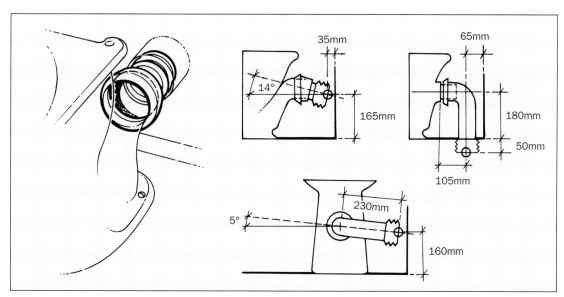

35mm

14°

165mm

65mm

180mm

50mm

105mm

5°

230mm

160mm

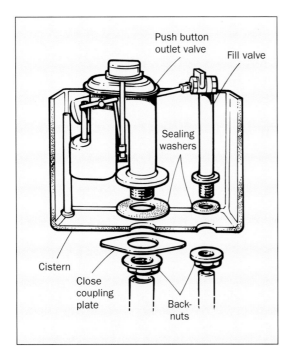

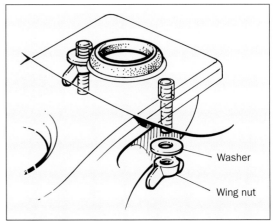

ABOVE: Follow the manufacturers' instructions to bolt the cistern to the bowl.

LEFT: Many manufacturers deliver cisterns with the fittings already fitted. Here a modern dual-flush-valve is included.

Plastic is generally used to manufacture the concealed cisterns that accompany back-to-wall and wall-hung toilets. The demand for concealed plastic cisterns in the bathroom has grown rapidly. Concealed plastic cisterns are usually fitted behind specially constructed partition walls and can also be installed within fitted bathroom furniture.

In the case of cisterns that are fitted into the wall or in furniture, some manufacturers supply a metal frame or 'in-wall' kit that is designed to carry the cistern and the flushing mechanism. This frame makes installation more simple and takes the weight of the toilet.

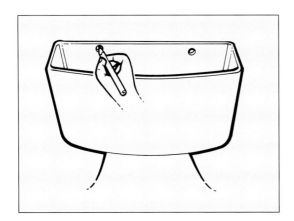

Carefully offer the cistern to the wall and mark for screw holes.

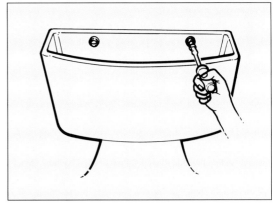

Finally, fix the cistern to the wall with brass screws.

RIGHT: Heavy-duty plastic cistern fixed behind finished wall – for use with back-to-wall models. (BMA)

FAR RIGHT: Metal frame used to fix the wall-mounted pan and concealed cistern. (BMA)

Cistern Fittings

Cistern fitting is the term used to describe the flushing mechanisms inside the cistern and the flush handles or plates used to operate the flush. There are a number of flushing devices used to control the volume of water used to refill the cistern after a flush has taken place, these include traditional lever-operated siphons and push-button operated valves. You can tell which type you are dealing with by the mechanism that you press. Siphons are operated with a lever; valves use a push-button.

Float-Operated Valves

There are two common types, one of which complies with BS 1212-3: 1990. Normally referred to as 'Part 3' valves, these incorporate a ball-float attached to a long arm. Part 3 valves are available in both side-inlet and bottom-inlet versions.

The alternative is the compact float valves complying with BS 1212-4: 1991 (*see* References for details). Also available in side- and bottom-inlet versions, 'Part 4' valves have a much smaller float and a shorter float arm than their Part 3 counterparts.

Float-operated valves are typically controlled using push-button flush-valves, which in most domestic situations are operated by manual push-buttons. To flush the WC, the valve's seal or stopper is lifted, allowing water to cascade out of the cistern into the WC pan. In many cases, WCs installed since 2001 will have two-piece buttons, the larger part of the button is pressed to flush away solid waste using 6ltr of water, while the smaller part is depressed to flush away liquid waste using 4ltr of water. In both cases, to give these valves the chance to operate efficiently and clean the pan thoroughly, I often recommended that the user hold down the flush button for around three seconds. Although most push-buttons are simple to operate, touch-free or extremely light touch flushing can be provided by electrically operated valves.

Siphons

Siphons have been used in the UK for over a hundred years. Typified by the flushing lever and the ball-cock inside the cistern, as the name implies they use a syphonic action, which, once started, discharges the contents of the cistern into the WC pan, creating a flush. Siphons have very few moving parts and are fail-safe in that they cannot leak.

For installations where easy flushing is required for the elderly, less able or very young, ergonomically designed flushing levers can be the best option. These can have an enlarged handle, so that the lever can be depressed with a wrist or elbow.

Silencing Devices

Some water-inlet valves are supplied with clear plastic silencing tubes that direct incoming water into the cistern below the water level. This reduces the noise caused by water splashing in from above, providing quiet re-filling.

A wall-hung WC
fitted to a metal frame,
positioned behind a
tiled wall. (BMA)

Back-to-wall WC
with cistern inside
storage unit. (BMA)

Toilet Seats

There is a lot of attention currently being levelled at toilet seats – their shape, their operation and even the ease with which they can be removed for cleaning, are all become factors of good seat design. There is even a move toward greater use of technology with oil-filled hinges that offer a 'soft-closing' action for toilet seats and ensure that the seat does not clatter when it is closed. Higher technology still has seen the design of a self-closing seat that lowers the seat and its lid as the user walks away from the toilet after use.

Styles of Seat

In more simple and mainstream terms, toilet seats are generally available in two main styles: round and elongated. It is important to make sure that the style of seat chosen is compatible with the WC pan, as they are not always interchangeable and need to be suitable for the proposed application. In the main, toilet seats are available in high-impact plastics and in a variety of woods. All but some specialist seats consist of a seat and a lid that sits down on to the seat. The wrap-over seat, as the name implies, has a cover that wraps over the seat to give a neater-looking appearance.

Fixing of the Seat

Toilet seats are hard-working parts of the bathroom and have to cope with constant movement and energy loadings in a number of different directions. In order to improve safety and to help reduce the risk of breakage, it is essential that toilet seats be fitted correctly and in accordance with the manufacturer's instructions. All of the fittings, such as fixing-bolts, nuts and washers, etc., are provided with the seat and all should be used in order to reduce potential movement.

NB A toilet seat is NOT automatically included in the sale of a toilet pan.

WASHBASINS

Shapes or Types and Sizes Available

There are five basic forms of washbasin:

- wall-hung basins, which are fixed to a wall using brackets for support, bolted directly to the wall;
- pedestal basins, which are fixed to a wall and also use a pedestal for the main support;
- countertop basins, which are fitted into a countertop by a flange on the ware, either on or under the countertop;
- semi-countertop, which are cut into the countertop but overhang at the front to form a design feature;
- vessel basins, which are bowls that look to be free-standing and sit directly on to a countertop or other mounting surface, such as a piece of furniture.

Wall-Hung Basins

Various types of brackets are available to support wall-hung basins. These includes basins fixed to the wall by screws or fitted on a dual towel-rail bracket or with concealed brackets. Whichever type is used, ensure the fixing method and the wall itself is of sufficient load-bearing strength. If doubt exists, another form of support such as a centre leg or pair of end legs and bearers can be used.

Wall-hung basin. (BMA)

ABOVE LEFT: Hand-rinse basin. (BMA)

ABOVE RIGHT: A pedestal basin. (Fordham)

LEFT: A semi-pedestal basin. (Ideal Standard)

Hand-Rinse Basins Hand-rinse basins are essentially small versions of wall-hung washbasins and are also available for corner fixing. Their compact dimensions make them perfect for use in restricted areas, such as cloakrooms. Because they are small and light, the support brackets tend to be more simple in design.

Pedestal Basins
Pedestal washbasins tend to be larger in dimensions with the additional weight being supported by the pedestal. The pedestal has the added advantage of concealing the waste and supply pipes giving a neater appearance.

Full Pedestal This is the most popular arrangement for basins in modern homes.

Semi-Pedestal This is a term to describe the wall-hung basins that have a matching ceramic 'half-pedestal' fixed to the wall to add strength to the fixing of the bowl, as well as adding styling to the piece.

Countertop Basins
There are three types of countertop basin: countertop, semi-countertop and under-countertop.

Countertop A full countertop basin is made with a flange that allows the basin to sit into an opening in the countertop. The joint should be made using a waterproof sealant.

Under-Countertop An under-countertop basin has a lip around the top of the bowl. This is to allow the basin to be fitted underneath the countertop using fixing clips.

Semi-Countertop In smaller rooms, a semi-countertop basin can be fitted. This is cut into the countertop but with its front portion projecting clear of the countertop. It is attached using small brackets supplied by the manufacturer.

Vessel Basin
Historically, this is the oldest form of washbasin with its roots in the old pitcher and bowl designs that

A countertop or inset basin. (Ideal Standard)

LEFT: *A semi-countertop basin. (Ideal Standard)*

BELOW LEFT: *An under-countertop basin. (Ideal Standard)*

BELOW: *A vessel basin. (Jacuzzi)*

predated the Victorian era. The modern-day equivalent is fitted with central drainage. Vessel basins are manufactured in a wide range of materials enabling more options in the design and fashion elements of the modern bathroom.

A vessel basin can be mounted on a variety of surfaces, e.g. sitting on a countertop, on bathroom furniture or simple shelving. Their simple lines make them a popular choice for anyone aiming for a modern look to their bathroom. There are many shapes and sizes of vessel basin and it is essential to follow the manufacturer's installation instructions, as fitting instructions can vary.

Fixing Washbasins

Wall-Hung Basins

For normal use, the correct fixing height for wall-hung basins is approximately 800mm from floor level to the front lip of the basin. Once the brackets are correctly fitted, the basin can be placed in position and checked for height and level. It is important to note that the manufacturing process of vitreous china is such that there will often be a slight distortion in basins. BS 3402 allows for up to 6mm on the level of fronts of washbasins (also on the straightness of pedestals) and up to 3mm on the back of washbasins which are attached to a wall.

Pedestal Basins

Because basins vary so much in size, shape and weight, this can only be taken as a general guide and the manufacturer's instructions need to be referred to.

Start by offering the basin, resting on the pedestal, to the wall and check that it is at the height indicated in the fixing instructions – check for level and then mark a line on the wall using the rear edge of the basin. Check with a spirit-level to ensure the line is level. Then use the manufacturer's template to mark the position of the wall-fixing brackets or screws. Alternatively, mark the wall through the holes moulded in the basin.

Once the basin has been accurately marked, offer the pedestal into place and, where the pedestal has fixing holes in the base, mark for floor-fixing screws using a pencil or bradawl.

> ### Choice of Tapholes
>
> Vitreous china basins are available with either a single tap hole for a monobloc mixer tap, two tap holes for fitting hot and cold pillar taps or three holes for fittings with an independent spout. The basins often incorporate an integral overflow, which connects directly to a 1¼in slotted waste fitting, with a separate plug and chain. Pop-up type waste fittings are available for added 'luxury'.

Move the basin away and drill and plug the wall. Take care to estimate the angle of the screw holes and angle the drill so that it matches the angle of the holes! This helps prevent cracking caused by uneven pressure as screws are tightened. The basin needs fixing to the wall for linear support.

If the manufacturer does not supply fixing screws or bolts, a heavy screw, say a no. 12, would be used for the wall fixing and a no. 8 would be sufficient for floor fixing. The taps and waste fittings should then

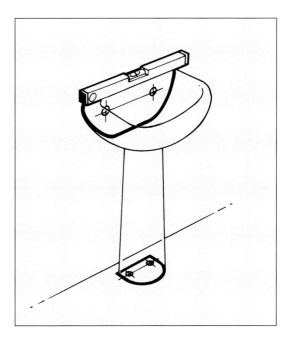

Fitting a pedestal basin needs some care.

Wastes and Traps

A trap must be attached directly to the waste outlet to prevent odours from the drains. The bottom of many traps are detachable for periodic cleaning. Alternatively, there may be a 'rodding eye'. Traps are commonly made from plastic because finish is not of paramount importance when out of sight. However, chrome finished or similar, can be used where the trap is visible to enhance appearance and to aid cleaning.

be assembled on to the basin as described in their individual instructions. Next, position the washbasin on to the pedestal or brackets and, with the basin in position, check for level and alignment against the wall and adjust as necessary before tightening any fixing pins.

Where the basin is moulded with screw holes, brass screws and soft washers should be used to secure the basin. Similarly, use brass screws and soft washers to secure the pedestal to the floor. Brass screws are used because the metal is relatively soft and will 'give' slightly as it is tightened. This makes cracking of the pottery much less likely than if a harder steel screw is used. Also, using corrosion-resistant brass screws will mean that the ware can be removed easily in future.

Where a pedestal basin has fixing holes in the corners, fit safety brackets with rubber-sleeved expansion bolts to secure it against the wall. This will help avoid creating strain on the supply pipes and waste.

When positioning the basin on to the pedestal it has become common practice to lay a thin bead of sealing compound to help to improve the seating. Finally, apply waterproof sealant between the back of the basin and the finished wall covering.

Countertop Basins

When fitting countertop basins, take great care to cut the opening correctly using the manufacturer's template supplied. Jigsaw blades are available that cut on the down-stroke only, this will reduce any chipping of a melamine finish that can occur with normal blades that also cut on the up-stroke. Alternatively,

stick adhesive tape on the surface, on the line of the cut, before attaching the template to get a good finish.

Once the opening is created, the exposed edges must be thoroughly sealed to prevent water damaging the chipboard. Two coats of varnish can be used for this. Where an under-countertop basin is to be fitted, even more care is required to achieve a good finish. Once the opening has been cut, an edging strip of melamine will have to be applied using a waterproof adhesive on to the exposed edge and carefully trimmed with a sharp chisel and fine file to leave a neat finish.

Countertop basins can also be fitted into other types of tops such as laminate-covered, marble, slate, stone, and so on. Once the opening is ready, apply a strip of waterproof sealant to the countertop surface and carefully fit the basin, before clamping it in position using the clips provided.

Use the Manufacturer's Template

Whatever the style, size or design of the 'countertop' washbasin, you must carefully follow the manufacturer's fitting instructions and use only the template and brackets supplied.

When fitting countertop basins it is essential to use the overflow fitment and all fixing clips and screws supplied by the manufacturer. It should be noted that, whilst most countertops are self-rimming for 'drop in' installation as per the template supplied, some designs may require, and are supplied with, fixing screws and clips.

BIDETS

The primary use of the bidet is to wash after using the toilet, either instead of toilet paper or as a final cleansing after using toilet paper. Formally described as a 'sit-on' washbasin, perhaps the best known description came from Paul Hogan in the film *Crocodile Dundee*, when he announced to the New York populace; 'it's for washing your backside'. Like water-closets, bidets can be floor-standing, wall-hung or back-to-wall.

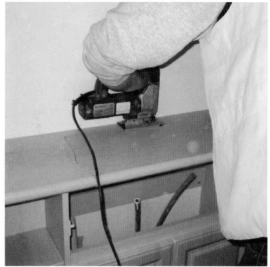

ABOVE: Perhaps the trickiest basin to fit is the semi-countertop, which requires some joinery skills. Start by marking-out, using the template supplied with the basin. (BMA – Shades)

ABOVE RIGHT: Cut the top and the unit front, with a jigsaw. (BMA – Shades)

RIGHT: Seal and fit the basin in accordance with the manufacturer's instructions. (BMA – Shades)

Types of Bidet

Bidets are available in two types: ascending spray and over-rim supply. The description refers to the way that the water is delivered to the area to be washed.

Over-Rim

In this type of bidet, the water is delivered from a tap in exactly the same way that water is supplied to a washbasin, so there is no risk of mains contamination.

Ascending Spray

This sprays the bits you want to reach with a shower of water. Because of the risk of contamination of the water supply, it is important that ascending spray bidets are correctly plumbed. Water regulations' permission is required from the local water supplier before installation of this type of bidet proceeds. Ascending spray bidets are becoming less common, in favour of the over-rim type.

CHAPTER 6

Brassware

Brassware has become the generic term that refers to all types of taps and associated fittings used on washbasins, baths and bidets to provide a controlled supply of hot and cold water from a household water system. Brassware items are generally made from cast brass with a protective covering of a harder or a more decorative metal – the term can also incorporate shower valves, which are manufactured in the same way.

The range of taps and mixers available to any potential user is vast and as styles, designs, finishes and fashions continually change, so do the types of products available. Whatever your preference, there will be a style, design, finish and a type to suit every bathroom application.

Brassware has been one of the primary indicators of changes in home fashions over the past decade, with designs moving away from Victorian

Modern mixer-tap with a softer styling. (HansGrohe)

styling with a gold finish to minimalist and cubist styling with a chrome or brushed-steel finish. In line with other home products, the more extreme minimalist styles are now being replaced by softer curves and a more 'human' style.

One of the characteristics of the bathroom tap or mixer-tap that is often overlooked is its performance, with many UK homes still not suitable for the Continental taps that are designed to operate on a higher pressure water-system. This book provides information on the types of taps available, plus their performance, and on tap installation. An appropriate degree of competence and knowledge of the laws and regulations, as they apply to installation of taps and mixer valves, is required; these regulations are in a period of change. In the case of any doubt concerning the installation of taps, mixers or associated products, the current water regulations should be consulted. Advice is also available from your local water company.

MATERIALS AND CONSTRUCTION METHODS

The body of a piece of brassware is formed from pouring molten brass into a mould, with a sand inner to form the waterways. The brass is then coated using electrolysis or, more recently, by bombarding the brass with a chemical coating that looks like the desired finish. Chromium plate is still the most popular but there is also a trend toward matt finishes like brushed steel or pewter.

MECHANISMS AND TAP OPERATION

Regardless of their exterior shape or form, the principals of tap operation are the same. They incorporate 'headwork', which controls on/off and flow rate. They take the form of either separate hot and cold controls, or of a single lever operation, where on/off mix and flow rate are achieved with one control. Taps with individual handles have 'headwork' valves that are available in two types:

• **Traditional rubber washer seal.** This type of headwork has been around for many years, it uses a replaceable rubber washer, and works simply by

Traditional tap valve. (BMA)

squeezing the washer over a machined hole to control the flow of water. These taps are available with a rising or a non-rising spindle.

• **Ceramic disc valve.** Ceramic disc headworks utilize hard-wearing ceramic discs that rotate against each other. The discs have a portion of their circle missing and when the gaps are in line, the tap is fully open creating a waterway. They have become popular due to their low

Tap valve using ceramic discs. (BMA)

Single-lever taps with a design difference. (Top and above left: BMA; above right: Ideal Standard)

SHAPES OR TYPES AND SIZES AVAILABLE

There are many types of taps and mixers available to cover all installations from the outside garden tap to the inside cloakroom, utility room and kitchen, through to the bathroom and *en suite*. Based around similar principals of controlling the flow of water, taps are chosen for design, cost, performance and installation requirements.

Pillar Taps

Pillar taps are used on sinks, washbasins or baths with two tap-hole installations. Available as a pair, these are designed to control hot and cold flow through separate units. Pillar taps are constructed with either size ½ threaded inlet tails for sinks and basins and bidets or size ¾ threaded inlet tails for baths. The differences in size of inlet and control valve reflects the fact that bath taps need a greater flow to more quickly fill the bath, than is needed from a basin tap.

Monobloc Taps

Designed for installation in a single hole in basins or in baths, monobloc taps are available with two-handle operation to separately control hot and cold water, or with single-lever operation, which controls both the mix of hot and cold water and the flow. Single-flow types allow the hot and cold to be mixed in the body of the tap. To comply with water regulations, such fittings require either balanced supply pressures or check valves fitted immediately upstream of the tap. Dual flow keep the hot and cold water separate until the point of discharge and therefore do not require either balanced supply or check valves. Monobloc fittings are usually supplied with copper inlet tails or flexible connections. They are designed in styles to compliment other bathroom brassware.

Basin Mixers and Bath Fillers

Two-Hole Mixers
Usually mounted on the flat sides of the bath, these taps can be supplied as single- or dual-flow fittings. Constructed with two size ¾ inlet tails, they suit baths supplied with two tap holes. Bath mixers can incorporate a hand held shower-head and flexible hose.

maintenance and ease of control, these headworks are available with quarter- or half-turn operation, from full-on to fully closed. The alternative to individual handles is single-lever operation often used with mixing valves. These also use moveable hard wearing ceramic discs, but the mechanics of the cartridge enable control of on/off, flow and temperature with the single lever.

Single-Lever Taps

Using a ceramic disc cartridge, some bathroom taps can control flow and temperature using just a single control lever – this allows some very imaginative shapes for mixer taps.

Modern pillar taps. (BMA)

RIGHT: Monobloc taps with two tap heads but the water comes from one spout. (BMA)

FAR RIGHT: Two hole bath mixer. (BMA)

Three Hole Mixers

These can be either basin types with size ½ connections or bath taps with size ¾ connections. Two individual side-valves complete with handles, control the flow to a central spout.

Four-Hole Mixers

This configuration is usually found only on baths where the hot supply, cold supply, filler nozzle and a shower-head attachment are all mounted in individual holes in the bath's rim.

Wall-Mounted Taps

Taps do not have to be mounted directly on to the bath or basin. Wall-mounted taps can be used where there are no tap holes available in the sanitaryware (e.g. 'Belfast' sink or a 'vessel'-style washbasin) or for modern baths. The wall-mounted taps are available in single- or multi-tap-hole configurations.

ABOVE: Bath mixer with hand-held shower. (BMA)

LEFT: The three-hole mixer tap is currently fashionable. (BMA)

BELOW: An additional shower-head converts this to a four-hole mixer tap. (BMA)

Two pairs of wall-mounted three-hole mixer taps adorn this modern bathroom. (BMA)

BRASSWEAR ACCESSORIES

Check Valves and Local Isolating Valves

Check valves (or non-return valves) are required to comply with water regulations with certain types of fittings. Check valves allow the water only to flow in the intended direction and are used to prevent 'grey water' or used water from baths, showers and toilets from flowing back into the supply system.

It is good practice to fit local isolating valves to all outlets, to enable local maintenance to be made without the need for full water shut-down. For instance, they may be fitted just beneath the toilet cistern, or under basin and bath-taps to enable easier maintenance. They operate with a simple half-turn using a screwdriver.

Pressure-Reducing Valves

In some rare cases, water pressure can be excessive. In such cases a pressure-reducing valve may be required. Check the water-pressure limits on the manufacturer's instructions or contact your local water company if unsure.

The arrow on this non-return valve shows water flow from left to right only. (BMA)

Pressure-reducing valve. (BMA)

SAFETY CONSIDERATIONS FOR HOT-WATER SUPPLIES

In modern homes the hot water is stored at around 60°C to prevent the growth of bacteria like *Legionella* in the hot supply. However, water at such high temperatures is a danger to bathers. Both the young and the elderly are most at risk because their skin is thinner and less tolerant to high water temperatures. We have enjoyed thermostatic controls in our showers for many years; more recently thermostatic devices have become available to control the outgoing water temperature into basins, bidets and baths. These units are known as thermostatic mixing valves – or TMVs – they are fitted under the appliance and connected to the hot and cold water. This is of obvious benefit to those preparing to take a bath. Despite recommendations to the contrary, most bathers fill baths by turning on the hot tap first. They then regulate the bathing temperature by running in some cold water. This results in a period during which the bath contains dangerously hot water.

The hot and cold water enters the valve and mixes to create the outgoing temperature. The outgoing temperature is usually set by the manufacturer, although it should be adjusted on site after installation. The regulation of the outgoing temperature is achieved by a thermostat in the unit, which keeps temperature variations to an absolute minimum, even when the incoming water temperatures or water pressures change.

There are two types of TMVs available and a risk assessment should be undertaken to determine which of the two approved product-types should be selected – TMV2 or TMV3 – for the particular domestic bathroom, dependent upon the needs of the user. For domestic installations, thermostatic mixing valves conforming to BS EN 1111 and BS EN 1287, with Buildcert TMV2 scheme approval, are normally selected.

Where there is a higher level of risk of scalding to less able occupants, then a thermostatic mixing valve conforming to BS 7942, with Buildcert TMV3 scheme approval should be selected.

One key safety feature on TMV2 and TMV3 thermostatic mixing valves is that the valves will shut off the flow of hot water in the event of interruption of the cold-water supply.

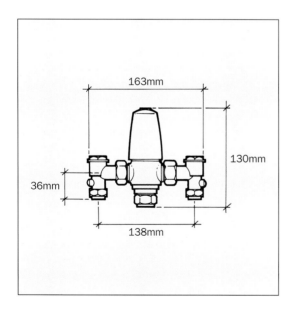

Thermostatic mixing valve.

Thermostatic mixing valve. (The Blue Book)

CHOOSING THE CORRECT TYPE OF TAPS AND MIXERS

Operating Pressures

With an influx of taps from the Continent, where domestic water-systems are totally different to the UK's and pressure tends to be higher, plus the advent of combi boilers being fitted into UK homes, which operate on the higher 'mains' pressure, choosing the correct type of tap is becoming more complex.

Historically in the UK, taps were required to work at pressures as low as 0.1bar. However, as new methods of heating water have been introduced, water pressures have increased, giving the consumer a much wider offering in terms of design and performance.

Operating pressure is the important term – it is used to define the pressure of water in a supply system (British Standard BS 5412 defines performance requirements for taps of the low-resistance type.).

The primary concern in the UK used to be ensuring adequate flow with low supply pressures. BS 5412 requires size ½ basin pillar-tap to deliver at least 7.5ltr of water per minute at a working pressure of 0.1bar. Such taps can be used with higher pressures but they will not need to be opened so far.

As already mentioned, 0.1bar of pressure comes from the stored water being 1m higher than the outlet of the tap. The water pressure in each home can vary and depends totally on the type of plumbing system installed. As a general guide, low-pressure systems have a cold-water tank in the attic and rely on the lower force of gravity to create the pressure at the tap – the storage tank is normally less than 10m above the tap, giving it less than 1.0bar pressure. In a bathroom, the distance could be much less, say, 2m or 0.2bar.

High pressure systems are mains-fed or pumped-gravity fed and can be 2 or 3bar or greater.

Before specifying a particular tap for use in the bathroom it is necessary to establish the type of hot-water system in the property. Specifically, is the water pressure high or low?

FITTING TAPS AND MIXERS

Before Starting

Before starting to fit any type of brassware, always read the instructions supplied by the manufacturer very carefully. Always make yourself aware of which side is hot and which is cold; usually hot is on the left and cold is on the right when viewing from the front. Always make yourself aware of where the nearest water shut-off point is, which can be a stop-cock or isolating valve. Its location is very important, as the fitting of any brassware cannot begin until the water feeding the tap has been turned off. If you have no localized isolating valves, it is always recommended to fit one near the tap – knowing its position afterward will help if there are any unforeseen leaks, or maintenance requirements.

Taps today are manufactured to exacting standards, so installation onto sinks, basins, baths and bidets is made as simple as possible. However, fitting new taps on to old baths can commonly throw up some installation problems. Tap holes usually measure 180mm from the centre of one hole to the centre, of the other hole; subsequently bath mixer-taps are designed to fit those centres. When fitting a new mixer tap to an old bath, ensure that the tap-hole centres are compatible. You may need to buy a tap with adjustable swivel unions.

Always know what your water-system configuration is (see Chapter 3).

Removing Old Taps

Once the water has been turned off, the taps can then be fully turned on and any drain-cocks opened to remove any water that has been left in the pipework. When the water has drained away, remove the old taps by disconnecting them from the water pipes, using a basin spanner to undo the tap connectors.

When replacing monobloc-style taps, disconnect the copper tails or flexible connections from the water supply pipes. Usually you will find that these have been bent during the original installation and need 'squeezing' together to get them through the hole in the basin or bath.

If a pop-up-waste is to be removed, identify the connecting clip that holds the vertical and horizontal rods together. Loosen the screws on the connecting clip and disassemble the rods. (Some rods, usually the longer vertical rods, may be made up of two or more parts – these can simply be unscrewed). Once the pop-up waste mechanism has been separated

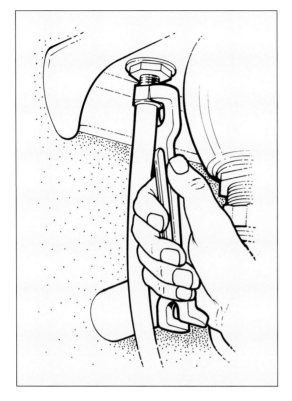

Use a basin spanner to remove old taps.

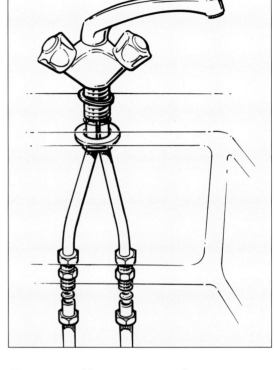

Fitting a monobloc tap.

from the tap, disconnect the waste pipe and loosen all nuts and seals. Use a basin spanner to undo the nut(s), situated under the tap(s). These may be individual nuts located on the threaded tails or, in the case of monobloc-style taps, it may be on a threaded stud, screwed into the base of the tap body.

Once unscrewed, remove the tap(s) from their holes and clean the surface around the holes ready for the new fittings. Cleaning the surface of dirt or old sealant, will ensure good purchase for any new seals. To clear out any swarf or built-up dirt, thoroughly flush all pipework after installing any new pipes or altering an existing system.

Fitting New Taps

Locate the new tap in the tap-holes, ensuring that some kind of anti-rotational washer or seal is fitted between the flange and the top of the ware. This may be in the form of a rubber/foam washer or 'O' ring.

Alternatively, bedding the tap on a bead of silicon sealant is acceptable. If sealant is used, this will take 24h to cure.

Once the tap is in place, locate and tighten the securing nut, pulling the tap down tight and compressing the sealing washer, if one is supplied. In some cases, a supporting washer or 'top-hat' may be required, especially where the thickness of a sink or basin is particularly thin. The supporting washer compensates for the thin mounting surfaces.

In the case of a single-hole monobloc-style fitting with detachable connections, ensure that copper pipes/tails or flexible connecting hoses are securely screwed into the tap body before offering the product to the ware. Make sure the copper pipes/tails or flexible connecting hoses are inserted through the tap-hole with care.

When the tap is properly fitted, reconnect the water supply, using new connectors or using the connectors from the previous tap but replacing any fibre/rubber sealing washers. An isolating valve should be installed to help with future maintenance, if one is not already installed. Standard connections for basins are usually 15mm × ½ (22mm × ¾ for baths). Various means of connection, including compression and push-fit, are available.

If installing a pop-up-waste, assemble the flange portion into the ware, ensuring any seals provided are in place or a bead of silicon sealant is used under the flange. Screw on the lower section of the waste, below the ware, ensuring that any seals are in place. Make sure the horizontal rod is pointing to the back.

Position the vertical rod down through the tap connecting any second lower part of the vertical rod to the upper part. Position the connection clip on the vertical and horizontal rods. Tighten the screws on the clip and check operation.

Final Checks

Once you are happy with the installation, it is now time to check for leaks. If you had to drain the system, be aware that air will be in the system, so when first turning the water on, you may hear 'spluttering and gurgling' or 'spitting' sounds. This will be short-term and should disappear after a few seconds.

COMMON FAULT DIAGNOSTICS

Most common problems that occur can be resolved after conducting a few simple checks.

No Water Flowing

- Is the water still turned off at the stop cock or isolating valve?
- Have in-line filters been checked for blockage?
- Is there an air-lock in the water supply?
- Have any non-return or check valves been fitted? If so they may be fitted the wrong way around for water flow direction.

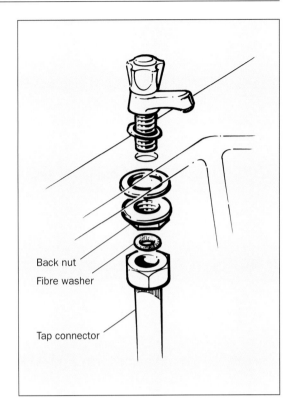

Back nut

Fibre washer

Tap connector

Ensure all relevant washers and clamping plates are fitted correctly and in place as shown in the fitting instructions.

Very Poor Flow

Does the tap meet the requirements of the water supply, with regards to water pressure and the minimum required by the tap?

Some taps are fitted with what is known as an aerator. This mixes air and water together to give a 'bubbly' flow. Aerators restrict the flow. Sometimes, these can be converted to become flow straightners, which provide less restriction (therefore better) flow, but the 'bubbly' stream will be lost. Check to make sure that all stop-cocks or isolating valves have been fully opened.

CHAPTER 7

Shower-Trays

Showers are perhaps the fastest-growing bathroom element being fitted into UK homes; they can also be the most complex part of the bathroom to understand and to install. Showers can be fitted over the bath, with a shower-curtain or bath-screen, or as a separate enclosure, or even as a complete wet-room. The majority of showers are made up of three distinct parts: the shower-tray; the shower-enclosure; and the shower-valve and kit; so that is the way we will look at installing a shower.

A few manufacturers make all three parts of the shower, but many more manufacturers supply just a single element. So it is perfectly normal to mix different brands of tray, enclosure and valve. In more specialist cases, where, say, shower columns are fitted, it may be better to purchase everything from one brand, if possible.

Within the whole process of buying a separate shower, the choice of shower-tray is often the part that gets least attention and yet it is the foundation piece upon which the success of the whole shower-installation rests.

MATERIALS AND CONSTRUCTION METHODS

There are six main types of materials used in the construction of shower-trays: vacuum-formed acrylic reinforced with fibreglass; stone-resin or high-density polyurethane foam; gel-coated or acrylic-capped; solid surface materials; enamelled-pressed-steel; fireclay. Always check the tray for colour, size and general acceptability before installation. Manufacturers are highly unlikely to accept claims for any of these once the product has been installed. It is common practice to fit the shower-tray before tiling.

Vacuum-Formed Acrylic Reinforced With Fibreglass

This is the same acrylic material referred to in the section on baths. The trays are moulded from acrylic sheet and reinforced for strength and rigidity; generally, reinforcement is provided by fibreglass – also referred to as glass-reinforced plastic (GRP) – sprayed on to the underside of the tray. The acrylic used to manufacture shower-trays is available in different thickness, typically 3, 5 or 8mm. As a rule, the greater the thickness, the less GRP reinforcement is needed on the underside.

Characteristics of acrylic trays are: lightweight; warm to the touch; easily transported; easily located and installed; available in a wide range of colours; hard-wearing; suitable for domestic use; excellent resistance to water-staining; available throughout the price range; up-stand options available.

Solid-Surface or Low-Level Shower-Trays

Solid surface describes a process where a liquid synthetic mix is poured into a mould, where it sets before the tray is de-moulded. This ensures that the shower-tray material is consistent throughout and produces a shower-tray of great strength. The minimum wall thickness of the material is likely to be 10 or 12mm and there is no need for any additional reinforcement.

The tray can be only 50mm in height and as solid-surface shower-trays can be installed directly on to a

Use of solid surface-materials offers a much lower profile shower-tray, where drainage allows. (BMA)

concrete floor or on to timber floor support beams, the step into the shower can be minimized by laying the flooring material and floor-tiles up to the edges of tray.

Characteristics of solid-surface trays include: available in unusual shapes and colours; available in low profile; can allow low-level or level access; warm to the touch; extremely durable; easy to install (low-level installation will need good 'joinery-type' skills); easy to clean and maintain; available at the higher end of the price range; resistant to staining.

Steel-Enamel Shower-Trays

Steel-enamel shower-trays are pressed from special alloy steels with low carbon content. They are pressed into shape and sprayed with an enamel finish, which is then fired through at temperatures of 850°C to produce a glass-hard, permanent lustrous finish.

Characteristics of steel-enamel trays include: abrasion resistance; impact resistance; heat-resistant; low expansion levels with temperature change; resistance to staining.

Stone-Resin or High-Density Polyurethane Foam, Gel-Coated or Acrylic-Capped

A surface made from a polyester gel coat or an acrylic sheet is put down first. A polyester stone and resin mixture is cast on to this surface to form a complete tray. This sets to form a strong durable product. Leg sets can be fitted to accommodate plumbing that is above floor level, if required.

Characteristics of these trays include: available in a wide range of colours and shapes to match baths; available throughout the price range; very strong; hard-wearing; heavier than an acrylic shower-tray; suitable for domestic use; straightforward to install; available with up-stand options.

Cast acrylic adds to the strength of this shower-tray. (BMA)

Fireclay

The traditional method for making fireclay shower-trays is to pour slip (liquid clay) into a plaster-of-Paris mould. The plaster absorbs most of the water from the slip leaving a firm clay piece. This is then removed from the mould, and trimmed and smoothed (fettled). The clay piece is dried in a warm air dryer and, when thoroughly dry, is sprayed with glaze. The piece is fired after spraying in a kiln, where temperatures exceed 1,200°C. This results in a robust ceramic shower-tray with a surface impervious to acids and alkalis. Fireclay shower-trays are not fitted with adjustable legs.

Characteristics of these trays include: available in a wide range of colour sizes to match bathroom sanitaryware; higher end of the price range; easy to clean; resistant to staining; long-lasting; fade-proof; resistant to acids and alkalis; suitable for domestic use.

SHAPES AND SIZES AVAILABLE

Shower-trays, irrespective of the material they are made from, are becoming available in a greater range of shapes and sizes, which are changing constantly. However, there are typically six basic shapes: square; rectangular; quadrant; off-set quadrant; pentangle; and off-set pentangle.

Modern fashions in the design of home interiors is bringing greater demand for new shapes in showers, with a growth in 'walk-in' showers and a flirtation with wet-rooms, as well as a number of 'super-showers' or 'wellness enclosures' offering all manner of therapeutic features, such as reflexology (foot-jets) and chromotherapy (lighting). So we can expect to see more designer shapes in the shower-tray.

TYPES OF TRAYS

No matter what the materials used or the shape, trays generally feature a mix of three basic characteristics related to installation needs:

- the kind of rim around the edge of the tray that is intended to help the seal with adjacent walls;
- the method used for standing the tray on the floor, either direct or on adjustable feet;
- the height of the tray, to enable water to drain away easily.

The Rim

This is referred to as either flat-top or up-stand.

Flat-Top
Flat-top describes a tray where the edge upon which the enclosure stands, and which butts up to the wall, is a flat surface.

Up-Stand
This describes a tray with a clearly defined up-stand moulded to the very edge of the tray to form a ridge that wall tiles can cover to provide a degree of flexibility to the seal. The photograph shows a shower-tray with an up-stand. The up-stand can be on all four sides or selected sides, as shown. This type of shower-tray is usually made from stone-resin or acrylic material.

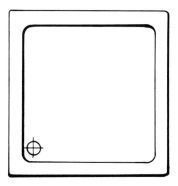

Square shower-tray. Sizes vary but 800 × 800mm and 900 × 900mm are typical.

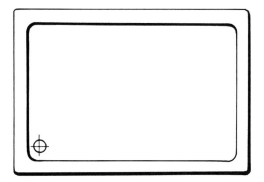

Rectangle shower-tray. Sizes vary but 760 × 900mm, 760 × 1,000mm, 760 × 1,200mm and 760 × 1,400mm are typical.

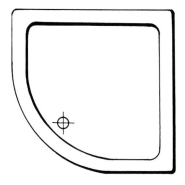

Quadrant shower-tray. Sizes vary but 800 × 800mm, 900 × 900 and 1,000 × 1,000mm are typical.

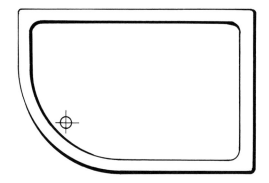

Off-set quadrant shower-tray. Sizes vary but 800 × 1,000mm, 800 × 1,200mm and 900 × 1,200mm are typical.

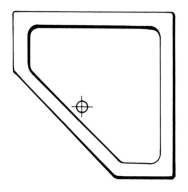

Pentangle shower-tray. Sizes vary but 900 × 900mm is typical.

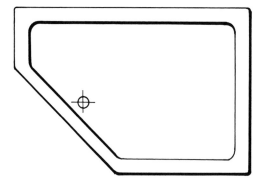

Off-set pentangle shower-tray. Sizes vary but 900 × 1,200mm and 900 × 1,400mm are typical.

Flat-top shower-tray. (BMA)

Up-stand shower-tray. (BMA)

By overlapping the wall tiles or other surface material over the up-stand, a more effective seal between the shower-tray and the bathroom wall is achieved.

Standing Method

The method used for standing the tray on the floor either direct or on adjustable feet.

Floor-Standing

The 'solid' materials, like fireclay, cast-resin or solid-surface, can stand directly on to a level floor. Where there is a need for more height to aid draining, trays are often set on a low platform at skirting-board level.

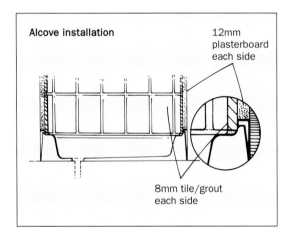

Cross-section that shows the up-stand of this shower-tray being set into the plaster, so that the wall tiles come in front, allowing a more effective silicone seal.

Risers

More and more shower-trays are becoming available with adjustable feet or legs; these are often called 'risers'. Adjustable legs deliver two advantages: they raise the base of the shower-tray off the floor; and they make installation easier, if the surface of the floor is out of level.

Raising the tray away from the floor will give the space needed for the waste-fitting and pipework without cutting into the floor surface, and will give the required 'fall' to ensure good drainage of water away from the tray.

Risers also allow for levelling on uneven floors – ensuring that the shower-tray is level is the foundation of good shower-enclosure installation. Riser shower-trays are available either with or without 'up-stands'; they are generally made from acrylic or stone-resin and supplied with matching panels.

Height of Tray

This can be either riser, standard height or low-level.

Riser Shower-Trays

This type of tray is recommended when the shower waste-pipe is above floor level. Height is adjustable but an accurate indicator would be 240mm, as shown in the diagram.

Standard Shower-Trays

The floor-standing diagram shows an example of a standard-height shower-tray at around 110mm. This type of shower-tray usually sits directly on to a floor, supporting the weight of the person showering.

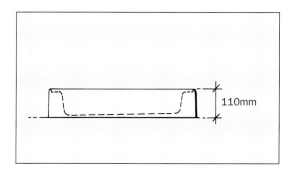

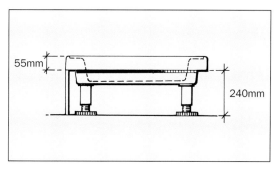

Cross-section through a shower-tray that is set directly on to the floor or a skirting-board height platform.

Cross-section through a riser shower-tray showing the adjustable feet.

Standard trays rely on being able to achieve the required gradient for the waste-pipe by running the pipes between the floor joists. If that is not possible, a platform must be built.

Low-Level Shower-Trays

Low-level shower-trays are approximately 50mm in height or less, and are made using solid-surface technology or steel. This means that they are extremely strong and are the same material all the way through. This strength means that they need no reinforcement on any flooring. Consequently their installation methods are different to standard trays.

By fitting this type of tray directly to the wooden beams that support the floor, the thickness of the floor boards plus the floor covering further reduces the vertical visual imprint, which allows these trays to simulate the 'wet-room' look and eliminate any step into the shower – provided, of course, that there is sufficient 'fall' to ensure adequate drainage.

SPECIFYING THE CORRECT SHOWER-TRAY FOR YOUR NEEDS

Riser or Non-Riser Trays

The first step of the installation is to decide whether you need a 'riser' (with adjustable legs) or a 'non-riser' (sits directly on floor) tray for your installation. To find out, answer these simple questions:

- Is the floor level (within 6mm across the length and breadth of the tray)?

Shower-tray in enamelled-steel fitted level with the floor. (Kaldewei)

- Do you want, or need, to position the waste and waste-pipe below or above the floor surface?
- Can you achieve the necessary gradient of pipework?
- How do you intend to secure the appropriate water seal?
- Will the user be able to easily step into the shower-tray?

Floor Level

Shower-trays are designed with sufficient fall in the standing surface to ensure that water easily drains into the waste outlet; the manufacturers expect that they will be fitted to a flat, even surface. You need to use a spirit-level to ensure a level floor; if the floor is out-of-level by 6mm or more across the tray length, using a riser tray (with adjustable legs) removes the need to level an uneven floor. In both cases, it is vital that the shower-tray base is supported in such a way that it avoids flexing during use.

Above Floor Surface

There are a number of considerations here, including the type of floor – is it wooden or solid? If it is wooden, do you 'want' to cut into the floor surface to position the waste trap and 40mm-diameter drainage pipe? Are the joists positioned in such a way to allow

a hole to be cut to fit the waste into the floor/timber/between the joists? Alternatively, would you rather install the tray and all of the piping above floor level?

Up-Stand or Flat-Top

The second step in making a choice on the type of shower-tray may be in deciding how the seal will be made to ensure that water does not escape from the enclosure. If you are tiling the walls within the enclosure, you may prefer an up-stand model, which is fitted so that the rim of the tray is recessed behind the tile face, thus helping to achieve a water-tight joint.

Height of Tray

One other factor you may like to consider is the height of tray that may suit your family best – particularly as there is a growing need for inclusive bathrooms. With larger numbers of us living longer, more and more of us will be facing the physical challenges of senior years in the coming decades. A recent survey by bathroom manufacturers highlighted a need for flat entry into the shower as an important factor; it is something that you may like to include in you plans for a bathroom that is likely to serve you for the next fifteen years or so.

The waste-trap is shown positioned above floor level. (BMA)

The wall covering is positioned in front of the up-stand. (BMA)

GUIDE TO INSTALLING SHOWER-TRAYS

The key elements to successful installation of a shower-tray are:

- a solid fixing that prevents movement of the tray;
- sufficient 'fall' on the waste-water drain, often requiring the tray to be raised;
- an effective seal to stop water leaking;
- a level installation to ensure no 'puddling' in the tray.

Remember too that the tray sets the foundation for accurate installation of the complete shower-enclosure that fits on to the tray. If the tray is out of level, you will forever be troubled by leaks, enclosure doors that do not fit properly, even cracked glass due to forces for which the installation was not designed.

Install the waste in accordance with the manufacturer's instructions, making sure that a water-tight seal exists on all drain connections. Be sure to provide access to the plumbing connections for future plumbing maintenance. It is vital that the whole of the shower-tray base is supported.

Tray Type and Floor Type (Room Considerations)

Determine the type of floor and consider each of the following.

Non-Riser (Wooden-Floor Installation)

Ensure that the floor is clean, dry, firm and level. If siting your tray on a relatively level wooden/stone floor, use a silicone-based 'adhesive' to bed the tray. Shims or wedges can be used for low spots on uneven floors. If the floor is a rough but relatively level stone floor, it is suggested the installer uses a purpose-made floor screed to smooth the area beforehand. Coat the ribbed underside of the tray with silicone sealant, then press down into place.

Position the tray to the walls and rebate the 'up-stands', if applicable, and tray walls into the plaster, as required. Bed the shower-tray on to a flat, even floor. It is essential that the shower-tray base is fully supported, using either sand and cement, in a 5:1 mix, or floor-tile adhesive. Coat the whole base area

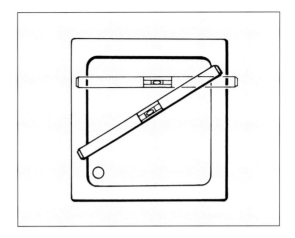

The shower-tray must be level on its top rim, or wherever shown in the fitting instructions.

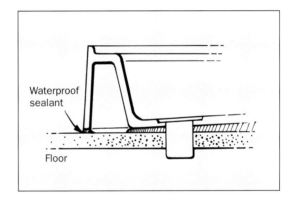

Coat the whole of the base to ensure full support.

of the shower-tray when sticking it down, with sand and cement or grout adhesive. 'Spotting' the centre and four corners is not a correct or acceptable installation procedure.

Ensure that the tray is level This is, perhaps, the single most crucial factor and the foundation of a successful shower installation. Primarily, that is because the bottom of the shower-tray has a built-in fall to allow for correct drainage. The manufacturers expect the outer edge of the tray to be installed level and the edges need to be checked with a spirit-level. If the tray is fitted out-of-level, the fall may be lost, which will lead to standing water being left in the tray. It will also cause tensions in the enclosure that is fitted on to the tray.

Connect the waste-pipe It is well worth spending a little additional time at this stage to ensure that you achieve a secure, waterproof and permanent seal when connecting the waste-pipe. It is a joint that you will not be able to see, it can do a lot of damage if a leak is left unnoticed and it is a lot of work to put right.

Seal the perimeter Seal the join between the shower-tray and adjoining wall with silicone sealant to provide a secondary seal. We do use a lot of silicon-sealing in bathrooms these days but do remember silicon sealer is not an adhesive, so do not rely on it for fixing. The seal will be lost if there is significant movement or shrinkage, such as that caused by settlement in new homes or ingress of water into plaster or timber studding from leaks.

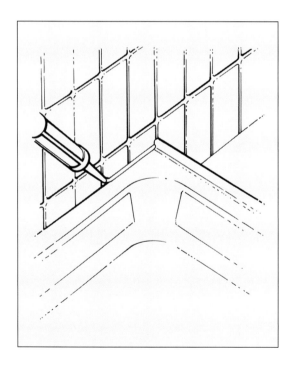

Seal around the perimeter.

Remove the protective film Acrylic trays have a 'cling-film' like sheet covering them. It is attached as a protection during manufacture and needs to be removed before use. It is not advisable to rely on this film to act as a protective layer against dirt, such as tile grout or adhesive, during installation.

If it is necessary to raise the shower-tray to accommodate the trap and waste pipe, construct a plinth, using timbers (75 × 100mm), with no more than 300mm between each timber. Finish with marine plywood base board 20mm thick. If a plinth is constructed, always bed the shower-tray to a plywood base-board, as you would to the floor, using one of the materials already described.

Riser (Solid-Floor Installation)
Refer to the individual manufacturer's installation instructions, as they may all be slightly different. To give you a guide, here is a list of the kind of steps that installation is likely to require.

Remove the base 'cling-film' The first step is likely to be to remove the protective film from the waste area and to the sides of the tray only. Leave the film intact on the upper surfaces of the tray.

Fit legs Fix the cylindrical locking nuts on to the adjustable legs. Set the adjustable legs midway on the leg moulding, this will give the initial clearance for the waste supplied. At this stage, do not tighten the lock-nuts. Fit the adjustable legs into the holes on the underside of the tray.

Offer the tray into position Temporarily fit the waste outlet pipework and the trap to the tray. Adjust the height of the feet to give the required clearance and ensure that the shower-tray does not rock. Position the tray up to the walls and rebate the tray and tray walls into the plaster (as required).

Ensure that the tray is level As with non-riser trays, the bottom of these shower-trays have a built in 'fall' to allow for correct drainage, therefore you need to check the edges of the tray with a spirit-level and, if necessary, readjust the height of the feet so that the tray is level in all directions, before tightening the

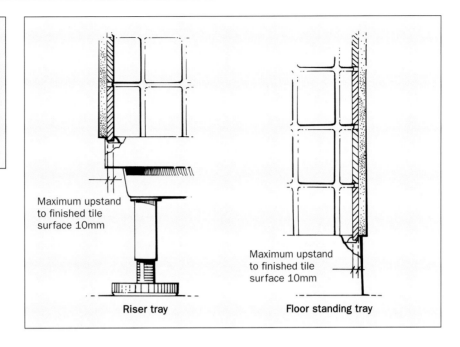

Tiling Tip

Do not tile onto the top of the upstand - flexing will almost certainly cause leaks. Tile in front of the upstand and seal with silicone.

Maximum upstand to finished tile surface 10mm

Maximum upstand to finished tile surface 10mm

Leave 3 to 4mm for final seal.

Riser tray

Floor standing tray

nuts. Once you are certain that the settings on the legs are such that the tray is level, tighten the individual lock-nuts on the leg-sets and tighten the waste, being careful not to over-tighten. Make sure that the seal is in place; additional beads of silicone sealant must be used.

Seal in place Check that the tray is firm and secure before sealing the joint between the shower-tray and adjoining wall with silicone sealant to provide a secondary seal. Check for leaks.

Finally, tile down to the rim leaving a 3 to 4mm gap between the tiles for sealant. If the tray has an up-stand moulded on to the outside rim, ensure that the tiles or wall covering is fitted over the front surface of the up-stand for a perfect seal. Seal the gap between the edge of the tray and the tiles with silicone sealant. Run water into the shower-tray and check for leaks before fitting any front panel to the tray.

Fitting Shower Panel

Riser shower-trays have a loose front panel (and, when appropriate, an end panel), in the same way that an acrylic bath has a bath-panel. The procedure for fitting this panel is quite straightforward, as long

as you remember to leave on any allowances for 'returns' before cutting the panel to its final length. A typical procedure for fitting a panel using double-sided adhesive pads to a square or rectangular tray begins by cutting the panel to length, ensuring

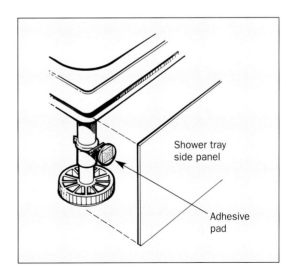

Shower tray side panel

Adhesive pad

Fitting the shower panel.

Trimming the Panel on the Shower Tray

The end-piece is designed to be used against a flat wall surface and cannot be cut. The panel, however, can be cut or shaped to suit any wall-profile, such as skirting board.

---

that you leave the amount of panel that goes into the 'corner connector' and the 'end-piece', if required.

Remove the backing from one side of each of the pads and stick the pads to back of locaters. Slide the locaters on to the clips, which are designed to be positioned on the tray's support legs. Slide the clips on to the legs until the bottom edge of the pad is 90mm from the floor. Where two clips are fitted on one leg, one of the clips can be inverted to allow both pads to be located at the same height. Make sure that they are parallel to the tray edge. Offer up the panel to the tray with the grooves nearest the floor and make sure that the panel is the correct length. If extra panel stability is required, secure wooden blocks or batons to the floor along the rear edge of the panel.

Remove the backing paper from the sticky pads and remove the protective film from the panel. If required, fit the end-piece on to the panel. Starting at the wall end, offer the panel up to the locater and press firmly. Continue along the panel, making sure that it sticks correctly. Fit the end-piece and the corner to the other panel. Fit the corner on to the fixed panel and continue along pressing firmly. Seal the top edge of the panel to the tray wall using a line of silicone sealant.

NB Please ensure that the tray is installed as per manufacturer's instructions. When purchasing your enclosure or tray, ensure that it is capable of coping with the water flow and drainage.

MAINTENANCE

Once installed, it is good practice to thoroughly clean the shower-tray with hot, soapy water and fully dry it with a soft cloth before use.

Many cleaners contain abrasives and chemical substances and should not be used for cleaning enamel or acrylic. These surfaces should be cleaned using a mild washing-up detergent or soap solution, rinsed and then wiped dry with a soft clean cloth.

The gel-coat surface on stone-resin shower-trays has good resistant properties to acids but should not come into contact with alkalis or organic solvents, such as caustic soda, dry-cleaning agents and paint-strippers. If in doubt, contact your supplier or the Customer Care Department of the original manufacturer.

CHAPTER 8

Shower-Enclosures

The second element that makes up a modern shower is the enclosure – the part that keeps the water spray under control and protects the fabric and the décor of the rest of the bathroom. Design in the bathroom is changing and, in the UK, use of the shower is where there are the greatest changes.

People use the shower in quite different ways now, even within the same family – some pundits believe that the use of the shower is becoming gender-related: men shower for speed and convenience, while women bathe so that they can pamper themselves with oils and scented lotions. Others tell us that the popular practice is to use the shower in the morning to refresh ourselves to face the day and then, after a day's work we pamper ourselves with a bath before relaxing in the evening.

There is a lot of evidence to show that different age-groups are embracing the shower for their own reasons. Older people, who may be unsteady on their feet, use a separate shower rather than stepping over the side of the bath, which they see as slippery and dangerous. Many obese people find it easier to step into or out of a shower-enclosure than they do lowering and raising themselves from the bath. Young, active teenagers use the shower several times a day, so that they can avoid the peer-pressure of unacceptable body odours. It is important to know how your own family uses the shower in the bathroom, so that the whole family can get the best out of it.

Also covered in this chapter are shower-screens that are attached to the bath – over-bath showers are still the most common form of showering in the average British house. As you will see, some bath-screens are now almost complete 'half-height' enclosures.

Once considered a luxury product, shower-enclosures have become an everyday product, with a host of manufacturers, all trying to be a little bit different, which means that there are numerous choices on the market. For example, some enclosures have thick wall-profiles with plenty of adjustment for fitting the screen to bathroom walls that are out-of-true; these are more forgiving for the less-expert installer or in older houses where walls may be out of true. Some modern designs, aiming for the minimalist look, avoid wall-profiles entirely or offer limited adjustment, which makes waterproof installation very difficult to achieve. Care should be taken when selecting a shower-enclosure to ensure that it matches the location and the installation requirements.

The amount of space that is available in a shower-room or *en suite* will often be the most important factor that determines which shower-tray and enclosure is suitable. Whether you simply want a shower-door to convert an alcove into a shower-enclosure, a two- or three-sided square enclosure or a different shape – curved, angled or rectangular – with the vast array of products available, most shapes can be accommodated, provided a suitable shower-tray is available.

It is important to allow comfortable access within the showering area to accommodate the door action, especially if selecting a pivot or hinged door that opens out into the room. Hinged, pivot, sliding and fold-in doors are available to open either from the left or right. Avoid areas where other bathroom fittings may prevent the door from opening fully. In cases where an off-the-shelf product is not suitable for the

customer's needs, then some manufacturers offer a bespoke service.

MATERIALS AND CONSTRUCTION METHODS

Shower-enclosures and screens are produced from a metal frame or supports – usually aluminium – and glass or styrene panels.

Characteristics

Perhaps it will be simplest to think of shower-enclosures in six types:

- **Framed**. The standard shower-enclosure, where the glass in the door is fixed into a metal frame.
- **Unframed**. Standard shower-enclosure but without the metal surround to the door. Frameless ranges began as top-market ranges but they are now available at lower price levels.
- **Walk-in**. Fully co-ordinating, frameless ranges, where the shape controls the water. Walk-in enclosures have no doors and they are becoming seen as

OPPOSITE: Framed enclosure. (BMA)

ABOVE RIGHT: Frameless enclosure. (BMA)

RIGHT: Walk-in enclosure. (BMA)

providing an adaptation of the wet-room look for the British bathroom.

- **Wellness or super-showers** offer an assortment of bathing options. They are normally supplied as a complete package with moulded tray and sides, integrated enclosure door and valves and jets. 'Wellness' refers to the number of therapy features, such as steam for relaxation and chromotherapy and multi-jets like the reflexology jets that direct water to the feet.
- **Wet-room**. The whole bathroom is sealed and water is allowed to run across the floor to an integrated drain. These are growing in popularity right now and are seen by some as a model for inclusive design, being suitable for wheelchair-users or people with age-related infirmities, like arthritis, who struggle with mobility and with grip on items such as small knobs on shower doors.

Wellness enclosure. (BMA)

Shapes or Types and Sizes Available

Basically a shower-enclosure can be considered to be four-sided and, typically, at least one of the internal sides of the enclosure is formed from the walls of the room. In most cases, the enclosure sits upon a shower-tray and, in conjunction with the wall(s) of the room, forms a water tight showering facility. An enclosure consists of either a door and a side-panel or panels – the doors can open normally, or they may fold, slide or pivot.

The latest trend in bathrooms can be seen to show us minimizing the shower-enclosure and moving toward wet-rooms or semi-wet-rooms. In some respect, by doing this, the UK is following fashions set on the Continent, where ceramic floor-tiles are the norm. As such, homeowners in countries such as Italy, France and Germany are not so worried if their shower-enclosures are not waterproof – a few leaks from the shower door is perfectly acceptable and many have a full-room drain to carry away any escaped water.

Although fashions for floor covering are changing, in the UK we still tend toward the cosier feel of a carpeted floor, which means that, for us, it is important that the enclosure does not leak.

Shapes

The shapes of enclosures largely follow the shapes of the shower-trays – square, rectangular, quadrant, off-set quadrant, pentangle and off-set pentangle – although it is not uncommon for enclosures to be described in manufacturer's catalogues in terms that refer to the balance between enclosure walls and room walls. They are often described as alcove enclosures, corner enclosures or peninsular enclosures.

- **Alcove enclosures**. Fit in the 'U'-shape created by three walls (back and two sides) and thus the enclosure to be fitted is just the front or shower-door.
- **Corner enclosures**. Typically there are three options, the most popular being a 90-degree corner enclosure, made up of a fixed side-panel and an opening or sliding door. There is also an

OPPOSITE: Wet-room enclosure. (BMA)

ABOVE LEFT: An alcove enclosure with framed sliding doors. (BMA)

ABOVE: A geometric pattern adorns this alcove shower-door. (BMA)

LEFT: This peninsular enclosure is unusual in that it has a curved door on either side. (BMA)

angled enclosure, where the door is fixed at 45-degrees with two side-panels. Finally there are curved or quadrant enclosures, the former having a curved door that opens as normal, the latter having a series of sliding doors.

- **Peninsular enclosures**. Just one of the walls is tiled, there are two side-panels and a door on the front – like a 90-degree corner enclosure but with two side-panels.

Decoration

Many attractive types of glass decorations are available, from elegant 'cut-glass' designs, simple modesty stripes to multi-coloured art deco designs.

Frames are available in a variety of coloured extruded aluminium profile, including silver, gold and white. Current fashions tend toward the simpler shapes and styles, with clear glass and the minimal amount of framing, or no framing, although this will inevitably swing back toward more traditional styling over time.

Over-Bath Shower-Screen

A common alternative to fitting a shower-enclosure and tray is to install the shower over the existing bath, and provide a bath-screen or curtain that is compatible for the shower. Screens tend to be more hygienic and efficient than a shower-curtain.

Different bath-screens are designed for particular baths or water pressures. When a power-shower is installed over a bath it is vital that a power-shower rated bath-screen or enclosure is specified. For an instant shower or a normal mixer-shower a single panel-screen should suffice, even so it is not unusual for some spray to escape into the room.

Baths must have a flat rim and should be installed with the top edge horizontal. Any water that collects around the taps should drain into the bath. The bath-screen must be fitted above the inside edge of the bath so it acts as a deflector and guides the shower spray into the bath. To maximize the shower-screen's effectiveness, run a generous bead of silicone to the wall-facing side of the fixing profile before it is screwed into place. Once the shower screen is fixed to the wall, you will need to apply a suitable silicone sealant to the inner and the outer edge of the wall-profile.

A bath shower-screen is often the most practical solution. (BMA)

The screen may leak if you do not comply with the manufacturers' installation instructions.

GUIDE TO INSTALLING SHOWER-ENCLOSURES AND BATH-SCREENS

Research indicates that most common complaints following the installation of a shower-enclosure refer to water leaking from the horizontal water-seal with the shower-tray or the vertical seal with the walls. Other common complaints are problems with the doors of the enclosure, which may not be water-tight or may be difficult to operate due to the structure of the enclosure being out-of-square.

In this guide to good practice for readers who are installing a shower-enclosure or bath-screen, we have seen that many shower-enclosures and bath-screens are available. It is important to remember that installation instructions can vary, even if the products look exactly the same but are produced by different manufacturers.

Before You Start

With some of the high-performance showers or multi-jet showers, the installer must ensure that the house's water-storage tanks can fill up as fast as they are emptied (because they can collapse if they do not), and check that the drain hole in the shower-tray can cope with the extra water throughput.

A power-shower can sometimes be fitted where other showers will not work. Even where the shower-head is higher than the water storage tanks, a special 'negative head' pump can operate effectively. It is important to remember that the shower-enclosure needs to contain the increased spray associated with a power-shower.

It is also important to remember that the showering area must be fully tiled and sealed to the shower-tray prior to the installation of the enclosure. The enclosure should be fitted on top of, and in front of, the tiled surface, and therefore, it is important to plan your enclosure design to be compatible with the measurements of the shower door and in-fill panels, if used. Consider access to the showering area, in particular if the shower door opens in, towards the enclosure, check that you have enough room to get in and close the door behind you.

The frame should have drainage holes or channels to funnel water back into the shower-tray when the shower is in use and side-panels must have a secure gasket. Doors should open firmly without vibrating or 'whipping' and should sit well inside the frame when closed, or leakage will inevitably occur. The opening/closing mechanism should be positive and firm, e.g. with a ball catch. Pivoting mechanism should be strong and long lasting – they are the only

moving part. Pivot pins should be made from stainless steel.

Unpack and handle the product with care to avoid damage to the product finish. Check that all the parts required are included in the product packaging and determine what additional equipment will be required prior to commencing the installation.

It is essential to check the product for defects, as many manufacturers do not resolve installation queries on damaged parts once the installation has been completed. Please ensure you read carefully and follow the installation instructions provided by the manufacturer of the enclosure.

Check for hidden electrical cables and water pipes in the walls prior to commencing any drilling work.

It is important that the walls are tiled after the tray/bath is fitted and grouted before fitting the enclosure/bath-screen. This will help provide maximum adjustment and will aid sealing. No attempt should be made to rework toughened safety glass.

Sealing the Tray/Bath

The tray should be fully sealed along the tiled walls prior to installation with a bathroom sealant. If installing a bath-screen, fill the bath with water and fully seal the bath along the tiled walls with a bathroom sealant. Once the bath is fully sealed you must leave for at least 24h prior to commencing installation of the bath-screen.

Note: Prior to commencing installation of the bath-screen, and once the sealant has cured, spray the shower handset around all joints to check for leaks.

Fixing the Wall-Profiles

To ensure continued efficient operation of the closing and opening of the doors, be sure to use a spirit-level when fitting the wall-profiles, which will secure the door or panels on the shower-enclosure or the bath-screen. The wall-profiles need to remain vertical throughout the installation procedure.

Fit the wall-profiles following the manufacturer's instructions. Always use silicone in accordance with the manufacturer's installation instructions. A good bead of sealant between the wall-profile and the wall will set the foundations for a perfect seal.

Follow the Manufacturer's Instructions

Experience has shown that failure to follow manufacturers installation instructions will result in incorrect installation and cause significant problems, the most common one being leakage. It is essential that you follow the manufacturer's instructions carefully.

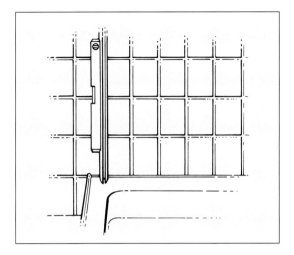

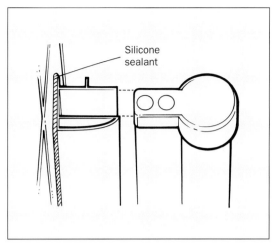

Ensure that the metal profile that holds the glass is perfectly vertical.

A good seal behind the wall-profile is essential.

The type of screw and wall-plug fixing that is best suited for your particular use will depend on the type of wall you are fixing the product to, and the weight- or potential weight-bearing capacity of the product you are using. Due to the huge variance of wall finish and condition in UK homes, not all manufacturers' products will come supplied with screws and plugs suitable for fixing in solid walls. When using fixings in solid walls, the hole drilled should be deeper than the plug by the diameter of the plug, e.g. for a 6mm-diameter plug, the hole depth should be the length of the plug plus 6mm.

Ceramic Tiles

You will need a special drill bit to drill through ceramic tiles. Once the hole has been drilled, insert the correct fixing. If you are using wall-plugs, make sure they are pushed in beyond the depth of the tiles.

Sealing Inside the Wall-Profile

After the wall-profile is secured vertically to the wall, use a bathroom sealant to seal the internal joint between the tray or bath and the wall-profile.

Applying the Seal Effectively

To ensure correct sealing of the shower-enclosure or bath-screen, it is essential that all seals are fitted as per

---

Drilling Wall Tiles

Place masking-tape on the tile where you intend to drill, this will help prevent the drill bit slipping.

---

the manufacturer's instructions. All seals provided should be measured correctly and cut to the length recommended by the manufacturer to ensure a water-tight seal of the shower-enclosure or bath-screen. Seals cut too short will cause water leakage, seals cut too long may affect the operation of the unit. Seals with a deflector must be fitted facing into the unit – this will enable water to be deflected into your shower-enclosure or bath-screen. Please note that many manufacturers supply seals that are the correct length and size, and will not require cutting.

NB Further adjustment may be required to ensure

Foundation of Successful Installation

A crucial element to the successful installation of a shower-enclosure is a level foundation (the shower-tray) – the second one being a good seal to the metal profiles that fix to the wall.

---

the seal is slightly depressed on to the tray/bath top.

Sealing the Fitted Shower-Enclosure/Bath-Screen

Once the shower-enclosure or bath-screen is installed, the final step is to seal the unit. To ensure a water-tight seal you must follow the shower-enclosure/bath-screen manufacturer's installation instructions. Applying silicone incorrectly or excessively could invalidate the manufacturer's guarantee and cause the unit to leak.

Please allow at least 24h for the sealant to cure.

SAFETY AND HEALTH

Shower-enclosures must be safe and strong and conform to BS 1474 with 4mm-thick toughened safety glass to BS 6206 to provide a robust and safe product. All glass panels must be toughened safety glass and carry a BSI Kitemark to BS 6206 Class A, and be a minimum of 4mm thick. Four millimetres-thick glass should always be framed, but glass 5mm or above may be unframed. The whole structure of the enclosure needs to be rigid to remain water-tight.

Fixing screws should be capped or covered with a panel, because exposed screw heads will deteriorate and lock, making future adjustment impossible.

The comments on safety glass apply to screens also.

For higher pressure showers, wider, two- or three-panel sliding screens are available. The first panel is firmly fixed to the wall and the side of the bath. The second panel overlaps the first panel until extended, when it is supported by the sides out from the first panel. If selecting this type of screen, check that all brackets or pins are metallic and that plastic components are non-load-bearing.

Cleaning and Maintenance of an Enclosure/Bath-Screen

Avoid using acidic based descaling products or products that are unsuitable for cleaning enamel surfaces, including abrasive cleaners or cleaners containing bleach or solvents, as these products will affect both the anodized and coated framework.

Never use scouring powder or pads or sharp instruments when cleaning the enclosure. Occasionally wipe the enclosure with a mild detergent diluted with water and polish with a soft cloth. If the installation is in a hard-water area, periodically clean with a 50:50 solution of white vinegar, soak for five minutes and remove any lime-scale residue by rinsing with warm water. Periodically clean the seals of the enclosure with an anti-bacterial spray. This will keep the glass, seals and coated/anodized aluminium parts looking as new.

Most manufacturers recommend specific cleaning agents, please refer to their specific maintenance and cleaning instructions, which they provide. Such products are tested with, and designed for, showering

CHAPTER 9

Shower Controls and Kits

The shower control, or shower valve, controls the delivery of water at the desired temperature via a shower kit, which comprises the shower-hose and shower-head. The kit can also include a riser bar, which holds the shower-head and allows changes in the height, plus a soap dish and a restraining device to prevent back siphonage. Speaking generally, the shower valve either heats the water at source or it mixes the hot and cold supply from the domestic system. Shower controls come in two basic types: electric showers, which could be crudely described as working like an electric kettle; or mixer valves, which work more like a very sophisticated tap.

BASIC SHOWER TYPES

Electric Showers
An electric instantaneous shower connects to a cold-water supply only. Models are available for both mains and cistern-fed water supplies. Electric elements in the shower heat the water as it is used.

Mixer Shower Valves
A mixer-valve shower connects to the domestic hot and cold-water system in the property, just as do the taps in the bathroom. As the name implies, it mixes the hot and cold supplies to achieve a preferred showering temperature. The flow rate from a mixer shower is dependent on the type of hot-water system in the property and the available supply pressures.

Generally, mixer showers provide a higher flow-rate than electric showers. However, where the hot and cold water supplies in a property are fed from a cold-water cistern and hot-water cylinder, the

Typical electric shower control with spray kit. (Mira)

pressure available to a mixer shower can be relatively low. To improve shower performance, a pump can be fitted. When a pump is fitted to the system supplying the mixer valve it is generally referred to as a power-shower.

MATERIALS AND CONSTRUCTION METHODS

Electric showers are produced from lightweight materials, the core components being the heater, the control board and the filter unit. Whilst the core material for a mixer shower is the heavier brass valve unit, in fact like taps, many people consider mixer showers to be brassware.

CHARACTERISTICS

Electric Shower

All electric showers use the same basic theory of operation. An amount of heat is provided from one or more heating elements and the flow of water is directed across these elements to provide the desired temperature. There are three basic operating types of electric showers (although new products are being introduced that may expand these categories). The three are:

- **Temperature-stabilized electric showers**. The desired temperature of the water is obtained by either increasing or decreasing the rate of flow across the elements. If taps are turned on elsewhere in the house, the flow of water is automatically adjusted to maintain temperatures within 5°C.
- **Thermostatic electric showers** incorporate more sophisticated temperature controls that can adjust the heat supplied by the elements. These shower controls maintain water temperature to within 2°C.
- **Pumped electric showers** include a built-in pump to increase flow rates. Pumped showers need to be connected to a water supply from the cistern and not from the mains.

Performance Characteristics
- Economical – heats the water as it is used, so no waste from heating a cylinder of water. An average

of five showers can be taken for the same cost as filling a bath.
- Easy to plumb in – requires a cold-water supply only.
- Thermostatic models available.

Mixer Shower

Mixer showers take the existing supply of hot and cold water, and blends them together to provide the desired temperature. Mixer showers can be described by their control configuration and whether they are set into the wall or fitted on to it (the way they look) and/or by their operating principles (the way they work).

Performance Characteristics
- Usually provide higher flow rates than electric showers.
- Ideal for homes with readily available hot water.
- Thermostatic models available.
- Options available for both low- and high-pressure water systems.

Mixer Shower Flow-Rate Characteristics
The flow rate from a mixer shower is dependent on the following factors:

- the available water pressures;
- pressure loss in pipes and fittings before the mixer;
- internal restrictions within the mixer valve;
- restrictions present in the shower-hose and shower-head.

It is important to ensure that water-supply pressures meet the specified running and static pressure requirements for the product; for instance, is the mixer designed for low- or high-pressure applications?

SHAPES OR TYPES AND SIZES AVAILABLE

Instantaneous Electric Showers

A wide range of electric showers is available and new models are being launched all the time. Apart from unique operating features for each model, electric showers fall into three distinct types:

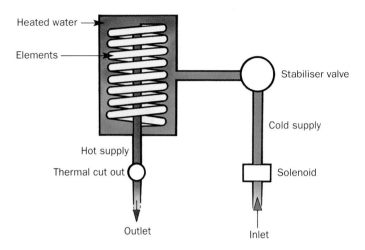

Heated water

Elements

Stabiliser valve

Cold supply

Hot supply

Thermal cut out

Solenoid

Outlet

Inlet

A temperature-stabilized electric shower.

- **Temperature-stabilized electric shower**. This type of electric shower incorporates a mechanical pressure-compensating (flow-stabilizing) valve. When pressure fluctuations occur in the mains water supply, i.e. when taps elsewhere are turned on, the stabilizing valve automatically adjusts to maintain the selected flow through the unit. If the volume of water passing over the elements is unchanged, temperature will remain stable. Typically, showering temperature is maintained to ± 5°C when pressure changes occur.

- **Thermostatic electric showers** provide enhanced temperature stability. Some incorporate sophisticated electronic controls to monitor and respond

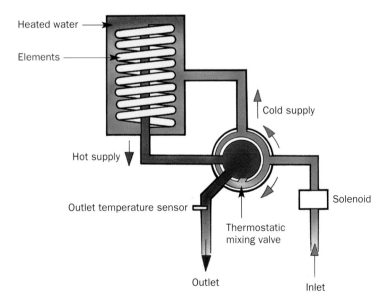

Heated water

Elements

Cold supply

Hot supply

Solenoid

Outlet temperature sensor

Thermostatic mixing valve

Outlet

Inlet

A thermostatic (wax-capsule) electric shower.

101

to sudden changes in site conditions, others use technology similar to that found in thermostatic mixer showers. Temperature is generally maintained between 1 and 2°C of the selected temperature when water pressure, voltage or ambient water temperature changes occur. Some models also incorporate a maximum temperature stop to ensure a preferred temperature cannot be exceeded.

- **Pumped electric showers**. Some models of electric shower have their own in-built pump. This type of unit must be connected to a dedicated supply from a cold-water cistern. They must not be connected to the mains cold-water supply. Having its own dedicated gravity-fed supply, this type of shower is unaffected by pressure fluctuations occurring in the mains water supply; therefore showering temperature is unaffected.

Both the temperature-stabilized and the thermostatic electric shower can also be installed to a pumped cold-water supply. The pump will be a single impeller type, which must be fed from a cold-water cistern.

Domestic Mixer Valves

A wide range of domestic mixer-shower products are available, all of which are constructed around a mixer valve, which, as the name implies, mixes the domestic hot- and cold-water supplies to achieve a preferred showering temperature. The type of mixer-shower products available are most often described in relation to their function, although they can be sub-described as wall-mounted or inset.

All mixer showers have a means of turning the flow on and off and regulating the hot- and cold-water supplies to establish a preferred showering temperature, but only some provide variable flow settings. Flow and temperature adjustment can be controlled in the following ways:

- **Sequential control**. A single control knob initiates flow at a cold setting. Progressive rotation of the control increases the temperature setting.
- **Single-lever control**. A single lever on the mixer performs two functions: moving the control up and down regulates the flow; moving it to the left and right adjusts the temperature setting.

Single-lever control in traditional styling – wall-mounted version. (BMA)

- **Concentric control**. An outer control knob is turned to initiate and adjust the flow of water, while a control within the centre of the flow knob is turned to the left or right to adjust temperature.
- **Dual control**. Two separate controls are provided: one for flow control; the other for adjusting the temperature.
- **Digital technology**. An electronic control-panel mounted in the showering area provides separate controls for flow and temperature settings, which can be programmed to take the individual user's personal temperature and flow settings.

Types of Function

Mixer valves are constructed as one of the following:

- a manual mixer valve;
- a venturi mixer valve;
- a pressure-compensating (balancing) mixer valve;
- a thermostatic mixer valve.

Manual Mixer

Manual mixer valves are controlled in the same way as a normal mixer tap – the user turns the knobs or handles that control the heat and the flow to their desired settings each time the shower is used. There is no further 'automatic' adjustment if the temperature, or the pressure, of water entering the valve changes. Manual mixers are best suited to balanced hot- and cold-water systems, where the hot-water supply temperature remains constant.

Concentric mixer valve – inset version. (Trevi Showers)

Dual-control mixer valve – inset version. (Trevi Showers)

Digital-control mixer valve – inset version. (Trevi Showers)

Venturi – Pressure-Boost Mixer Shower

The venturi mixer shower is specifically designed to work on unbalanced supplies of mains cold water at a higher pressure, and gravity-fed hot water at a lower pressure. Some describe it as a half-way house to a power-shower because a venturi mixer uses the extra pressure of the cold water to significantly increase the flow rate of hot water, using the venturi principle.

In other words, as the cold water passes through the specially shaped venturi, its velocity increases and this causes a suction effect that pulls the hot water through the valve at a greater rate of flow. As the mixed water leaves the venturi, it flows at a level significantly higher than the hot supply was on entry, thereby providing a forceful shower.

For correct operation of a venturi or boost shower valve, the mains cold-water pressure must be at the minimum running pressure specified by the manufacturer, usually around 1.5bar. In some cases where water pressure is excessive, a pressure-reducing valve needs to be fitted to limit pressure to 3bar. To comply with water regulations, check valves are required on both the hot and cold supplies to ensure no back-flow can occur.

Pressure-Compensating (Balancing) Mixer Valve

This type of mixer provides greater temperature stability compared to a manual mixer. Some are designed for both low- and high-pressure systems, others for high-pressure systems only. Mixers are produced with either sequential or dual controls to set the flow and temperature.

Sequential control starts the shower at a cold setting. Turning the control progressively increases showering temperature, whilst maintaining a relatively fixed flow rate.

Dual control pressure-compensating mixers have a separate flow-control (tap) and temperature-control (pressure compensating) mechanism.

Pressure-compensating mixers maintain showering temperature when pressure changes occur in the supplies. However, they cannot react to changes in supply temperature; therefore they should only be installed on hot-water systems that maintain a stable delivery temperature.

Thermostatic Mixer Valves

Thermostatic mixers maintain the set temperature when pressure or temperature changes occur in the water supplies. They also afford the added safeguard of shutting off flow should there be a total loss of either supply. The maximum temperature that can be selected may be factory-set by the manufacturer, and is normally between 38 and 41°C. There will usually be some means of internal adjustment or an external pushbutton temperature over-ride, allowing selection of hotter settings. Valves that have been factory-set are calibrated on the basis that water entering the mixer will be approximately 55°C hot and 15°C cold. Following installation, a minor adjustment of the temperature stop may be necessary to suit the available supply conditions. Having set a showering temperature, a thermostatic device in the mixer valve maintains that temperature.

Pressure (Flow Rate)

Low-Pressure Mixing Valves

Low-pressure mixer valves are designed for use on gravity-fed systems where pressures are between 0.1 to 1bar. If dealing with a low-pressure installation, keep any restrictions, such as elbow joints and bends, to a minimum. In extreme cases, to achieve the required minimum running pressure of 0.1bar at the valve, it may be necessary to raise the cold-water cistern or increase the size of pipe and fittings to reduce frictional losses. Because of the difficulties involved in raising a cold-water cistern, it has become more common to increase gravity system pressure by installing a booster pump. If the minimum specified running pressure is achieved at the mixer valve, flow rates should be near to those quoted by the manufacturer. Performance will vary from one mixer to another, as restrictions within each valve and showerhead can differ.

High-Pressure Mixing Valves

Some valves are designed for use on pumped gravity and mains-fed water systems only, where the minimum pressure is 1bar. High-pressure valves are generally designed to be more restrictive to provide better control of flow and temperature at the higher pressures. Flow rates in excess of 20ltr/min can be achieved, depending on available water pressure and mixer design.

General Purpose Mixing Valves

Some mixer valves are designed to work on all types of plumbing system, i.e. balanced gravity systems from 0.1 to 1bar and pressurized systems above 1bar. Some general purpose mixers are specified for connection to mains-fed cold water and gravity-fed hot water. However, it should be noted that an imbalance of pressure outside the ratio stated by the manufacturer could give rise to fluctuations in showering temperature.

To comply with water regulations, check valves must be present in both supplies to prevent cross-flow through the mixing valve.

Power-Shower

Often perceived to be the ultimate in exhilarating shower performance with high-pressure spray or sprays from gravity-fed water supplies using a pump to boost the flow. The pump can be integrated within the shower unit or may be a separate pump and mixer valve. Thermostatic models are available.

SPECIFYING THE CORRECT SHOWER CONTROL FOR YOUR NEEDS

The 'Rate Your Bathroom' section in Chapter 2 will help you to decide the kind of shower control that will best fit your life-style. You will also need to refer to Chapter 3 to help you to identify your own home's water system before choosing a control that will deliver the performance you desire.

Many of the top valve manufacturers offer additional guidance in their brochures and on their websites or via their customer care departments. In all cases the manufacturer's guidance on plumbing requirements must be followed.

GUIDE TO INSTALLING ELECTRIC SHOWER VALVES

Installing Mains-fed Electric Showers

Most electric showers simply connect to the mains cold-water supply. Electric showers require an adequate pressure to activate a pressure or flow switch in the unit that controls the heater circuits and flow of water, to allow optimum performance all year round. This minimum pressure/flow is required to enable the water flow through internal restrictions such as the solenoid valve, stabilizer valve and heater assembly. Pressure and flow requirements will vary according to the model selected and its kilowatt rating. The specification supplied with each model states the required minimum running pressure and flow, and the maximum acceptable static pressure.

The pressure referred to is that which is present at the inlet to the unit whilst it is in use (running pressure) or when it is turned off (static pressure). Water pressure varies during the day, being at its lowest pressure at the time of peak demand. Thus, ideally, static pressure should be measured at the time of off-peak demand, and running pressure at the time of peak demand. Typically, running water pressure

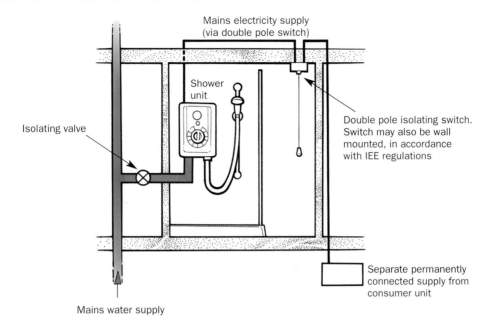

Mains electricity supply
(via double pole switch)

Shower
unit

Isolating valve

Double pole isolating switch.
Switch may also be wall
mounted, in accordance
with IEE regulations

Separate permanently
connected supply from
consumer unit

Mains water supply

Electric shower connected to the cold-water supply.

requirements are between 0.8 and 1.5bar. The maximum static pressure rating is usually between 8 and 10bar. Where mains water pressure is inadequate or erratic, a pumped electric shower can be installed. These must be connected to a cistern (tank) fed water supply only.

Installing Pumped Electric Showers

There are two types of pumped electric shower installation: an electric shower connected to a remote single impeller pump; and an electric shower with its own built-in pump. In both cases, to comply with the water regulations/bye-laws, the water must be supplied from a cold-water cistern.

Single Impeller Pump

A single impeller pump can be located in an airing cupboard or other suitable location remote from the showering area. In most cases, the pump will be fitted with a flow switch that starts the pump whenever the shower unit is turned on. The pump will stop when the shower is turned off. If the minimum head of water needed to operate the flow switch cannot be achieved, a momentary action switch may be required.

In cases where the cold-water cistern is below the level of the shower-head a negative-head pump will be required. This type of pump has a negative head (pressure switch) to start the pump and push water up to the shower. When the shower is turned off, the pump continues to run for a second or two until sufficient pressure builds up in the pipework to operate the negative-head switch and turn the pump off.

Built-In Pump

An electric shower with its own built-in pump must be connected to a cistern with its base above the top of the shower unit in order to fill and prime the shower with water Check individual fixing instructions for minimum height required.

This type of unit offers certain advantages: there is no need to find a suitable location for a separate pump and there is only one electric circuit to install instead of two. In either case, the cold supply must come from a dedicated connection to the cold-water cistern. To avoid drawing air into the pump, the connection should be on the opposite side to the float-operated valve that fills the cistern.

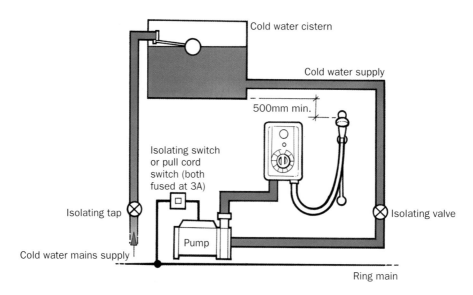

Electric shower with separate pump.

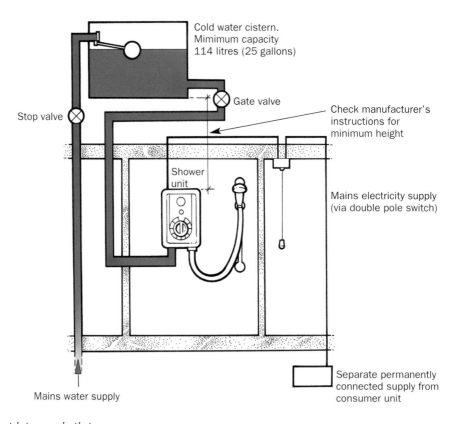

Electric shower with its own built-in pump.

Note: The flow rate from a pumped electric shower is no different to an electric shower connected to the mains cold-water supply and the flow must still be adjusted relative to the ambient water temperature and kW rating of the elements.

Do not mistake this type of unit for a power-shower, which is comprised of a mixer valve and pump arrangement.

General Installation Guidance
Once the method of supplying the shower with water is established, the connections may be completed using normal plumbing methods. The final connection to the shower unit must be made using the manufacturers' recommended type of fitting. It is advisable not to use solder fittings in close proximity to the shower unit, to avoid damage from heat.

Jointing compound should not be used on any pipe or fittings in the installation, as this can block the inlet filter in the shower. It is essential that pipework is flushed out before finally fitting of the unit – failure to do so can result in debris blocking filters or entering the unit and damaging internal parts.

A suitable isolating valve must be fitted in the supply to the shower to enable future maintenance and servicing. Non-restrictive full-way isolating valves are recommended, particularly where site pressures are low.

If the shower-head can be removed from its holder and lowered to within 25mm of the rim of a bath or shower-tray, then some means of back-flow prevention (anti-siphon device) must be fitted to comply with the water regulations. This may be a double check valve fitted in the supply to the shower or, alternatively, an anti-siphon fitting designed to go on the outlet of the shower.

Always follow the manufacturer's guidance on acceptable fittings for their showers.

Electrical Requirements
From January 2005 all new electrical installations in domestic dwellings must comply with Part P of the Building Regulations. If installation is carried

Flush out the pipes to keep the installation dirt from contaminating the valve.

out by anyone who is not registered to self-certificate electrical work, then the Building Control Office must be notified before work commences.

Setting Up the New Shower
It is essential to commission any shower in accordance with the manufacturer's instructions. Failure to do so can result in damage to the heater assembly. In all cases it is necessary to ensure that the heater is filled with water before switching on the elements.

When filling the unit, the shower-hose can be fitted but the shower-head must be left off. This ensures back-pressure is not created inside the unit, which could cause the pressure-relief device in the shower to operate.

Power Required
A unit of 7.0kW rating will draw 30A.
A unit of 7.5kW rating will draw 32A.
A unit of 8.0kW rating will draw 33.3A.
A unit of 8.5kW rating will draw 35.4A.
A unit of 9.5kW rating will draw 39.6A.
A unit of 10.5kW rating will draw 43.75A.

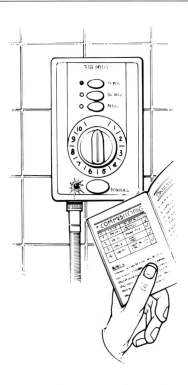

Take care in initially setting up the new shower to avoid possible damage.

GUIDE TO INSTALLING MIXER VALVES

The requirement of any mixer shower is that it blends hot and cold water to achieve a comfortable shower temperature. The first factor to establish in choosing the type of shower for your home, is the type of water system you have.

The recommended hot-water temperature to be supplied to a mixer valve is between 55 and 65°C. The boiler in the house – or other water-heating appliance – must be capable of supplying at least 52°C at flow rates between 3 and 8ltr/min. If mixer valves are subjected to temperatures above 80°C, there is a likelihood that internal components may be damaged. In the case of thermostatic mixer valves, depending on the customer's requirements and variations in hot-water supply temperatures, it may be necessary to adjust the maximum temperature stop from its factory set position. Before advising on adjustment, always refer to the commissioning section in the relevant fitting instructions.

In most cases, the hot- and cold-water pressures must be nominally equal and within the mixer valve's specified operating range, i.e. low pressure 0.1 to

---

Electric Showers – Common Site Problems – Causes and Remedies

When certain problems arise it is advisable to check the following points:

Symptom: Water is flowing but it is not being heated.
Causes and remedies: Insufficient water pressure to activate the pressure switch in the shower; restrictions in the cold supply, reducing pressure to the shower – check isolating valves are fully open and the filter in the shower is not blocked.

Water supply pressure does not meet minimum switch-on requirement – re-plumb to a pumped supply.

Symptom: Shower temperature is too hot.
Causes and remedies: It could be a restriction on the outlet of the shower limiting flow through the heater – check that the shower-head is not blocked and that the shower-hose is not twisted inside.

It could be a restriction in the cold supply limiting flow through the shower – check isolating valves are fully open and the filter in the shower is not blocked.

Symptom: Shower will not switch on.
Cause and remedy: It could be a loose electrical connection in the circuit – check connections in consumer unit, double pole isolating switch and terminal block in shower.

Symptom: Shower will not shut off flow.
Cause and remedy: Filter has not been fitted in the shower inlet resulting in debris damaging the flow shut-off valve – replace damaged flow shut-off valve and flush out pipes before reconnecting the shower.

1bar, high pressure greater than 1bar running pressure. If pressures exceed the specified maximum running pressure, then a pressure-reducing valve must be fitted. In domestic installations this is best set to around 3.5bar running pressure.

Gravity-Fed Hot-Water System

Mains cold water is supplied into a storage cistern via a float-operated valve. Connections at the base of the cistern distribute water to supply, in some cases, both hot and cold taps within the property. Alternatively, the cistern will supply the hot-water cylinder only, the cold water taps being connected to the mains cold-water supply.

In either case, the domestic hot-water circuit is the same. Water from the cistern is delivered into the bottom of the hot-water cylinder. When full, water flows out from a connection at the top of the hot-water cylinder. Pipework from this point distributes water to the hot taps within the property. An open section of pipe also rises above the cistern to maintain stored water at atmospheric pressure with a boiling point of 100°C. Cylinder capacities vary – in domestic dwellings, the cylinder will usually contain 115 to 230ltr of stored water heated to between 60 and 65°C.

The most common gravity system consists of a cistern located in the roof space approximately 2m above the cylinder in an airing cupboard. Other arrangements exist in the form of combination cylinders, which consist of a small cold-water cistern and hot-water cylinder in a single compact unit. This type of arrangement is usually unsuitable for mixer valve showers due to the limited volume of stored cold water and the lack of head pressure available.

In a gravity-fed system, flow rate is determined by two factors: the height of the cold-water cistern above the shower spray; and restrictions within the system, i.e. pipe, fittings, valves and shower-head. For water to be forced out of the system, a head of water must exist. Head is the vertical measurement from the base of the cistern to the shower-spray. Every 1m head achieved will result in a pressure increase of 0.1bar.

Information on Pressure

10m head = 1bar = 100kPa.

Suitable Shower Types for a Gravity System

- Manual mixer valves.
- Venturi mixer showers.
- LP and GP thermostatic mixer valves.
- LP and GP bath mixer showers.
- Twin-ended pumps.
- Integral pump power-showers.
- Pumped shower panels.

In domestic situations, head of water may be less than 1m, therefore minimal pressure exists to force water through the system. In addition to the low head factor, restrictions within the system will reduce the pressure further. As the water flows through fittings and valves, etc., a pressure loss occurs; if these areas are particularly restrictive, pressure and flow at the shower-head can be negligible.

By ensuring restrictions are kept to a minimum, i.e. limiting the use of 90-degree elbows and forming gentle bends in pipes wherever possible, acceptable performance can be achieved. Considering all factors, flow rates from gravity-fed mixer showers will be around 5ltr/min and can peak at 8ltr/min.

Pumped Gravity Shower Systems

Installing a booster pump will improve gravity system pressure and the performance of mixer showers. In domestic situations a pump can be installed to improve flow rate from a number of outlets, but more common is the installation of a pump to boost the pressure and flow from a single mixer shower, bath shower mixer or shower panel. It is important to note that shower booster pumps must not be connected to mains-fed hot or cold supplies, as this contravenes water regulations. Also, there is real risk that mains pressure will damage the pump.

All shower pumps must be installed below the bottom of the cold-water cistern, so that the pump chamber(s) can fill with water. Turning on a pump before it has been primed with water will damage the internal seals. There are three types of pump that are suitable for shower applications: single-ended pump; twin-ended pump; integral-pump mixer.

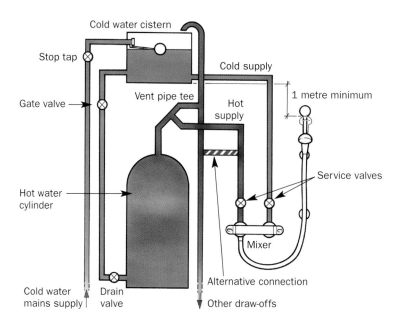

Mixer shower valve fitted in a gravity-fed water system.

Single-Ended Pump

This pump consists of a single pumping chamber with one or more impellers and must be installed between the mixer and the shower-head. The pump may be fitted with a flow switch on the outlet, to start the pump when the mixer is turned on. Blended water is then delivered directly to the shower-head. When the mixer valve is turned off, the flow switch is de-activated and the pump stops running. Some pumps can be wall-mounted in the showering area; in which case the pump is turned on and off by a start/stop switch on the unit.

Twin-Ended Pump

A twin-ended pump has two pumping chambers, each with one or more impellers. One chamber is used to pump cold water, the other to pump hot water. The pump is fitted in the water supply between the stored water and the mixer shower. Typical locations being in an airing cupboard or under a bath. A flow or pressure switch on the pump is activated when the mixer shower is turned on; hot and cold water is then supplied to the shower at increased pressure.

For a flow switch to operate there must be a positive head of water above the shower-head. If the shower manufacturer's head requirement cannot be met, or there is a negative head situation, then a negative-head (pressure) switch, air switch or momentary pull-cord switch will be required to start the pump. Providing that independent supplies of hot and cold water have been taken to the pump, then balanced pressures will be maintained whilst showering.

Check with manufacturers to ascertain which mixer valves are suitable for a pumped shower. High-pressure thermostatic mixing valves and bath shower mixers; general purpose thermostatic mixing valves and bath shower mixers; pressure-compensating mixer valves; manual mixer valves and shower panels, should all be suitable for installation with a pump.

Integrated-Pump Shower

In this type of shower, both the pump and mixer valve are housed within a wall-mounted unit, for installation in the showering area. A single-ended pump in the unit draws water through a mixer valve,

110

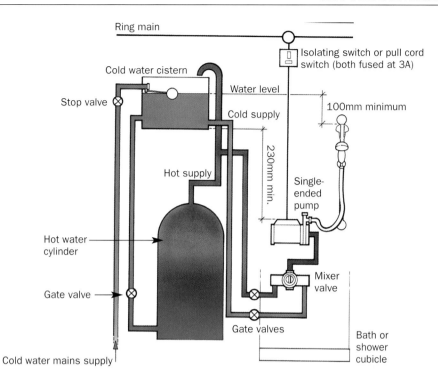

Ring main

Isolating switch or pull cord
switch (both fused at 3A)

Cold water cistern

Water level

100mm minimum

Stop valve

Cold supply

230mm min.

Hot supply

Single-
ended
pump

Hot water
cylinder

Mixer
valve

Gate valve

Bath or
shower
cubicle

Gate valves

Cold water mains supply

Single-ended pump fitted to boost shower pressure.

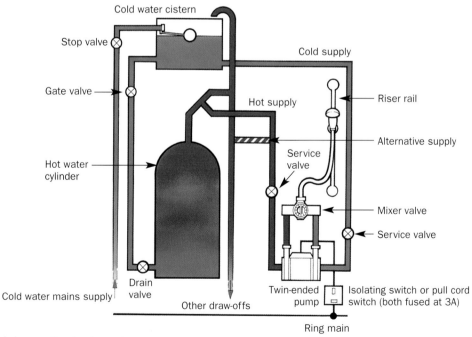

Cold water cistern

Stop valve

Cold supply

Gate valve

Hot supply

Riser rail

Alternative supply

Service
valve

Hot water
cylinder

Mixer valve

Service valve

Drain
valve

Twin-ended
pump

Isolating switch or pull cord
switch (both fused at 3A)

Cold water mains supply

Other draw-offs

Ring main

Twin-ended pump fitted to boost shower pressure.

111

which can be manual or thermostatic in operation, and delivers it to the shower-head at the selected temperature and flow rate. This type of shower does not require a flow or pressure switch to start the pump, as it can be operated by a start/stop switch on the unit.

Providing the unit is located under the level of the cold-water cistern, sufficient to flood the pump chamber, it is possible to position the shower-head above the height of water in the cistern. This can be of benefit in properties where the cold-water cistern is in an airing cupboard and there is minimal head of water above the top of the unit.

It is best practice to connect this type of shower to independent hot- and cold-water supplies. Connecting to pipes supplying other outlets can result in the pump being starved of water when the other outlets are in use.

Pump-Performance Characteristics

Domestic shower pumps are designed to improve gravity-fed 15 or 22mm supplies to showers. Pump performance is such that when very little flow is taking place at the terminal fitting, the pressure inside the pumping chamber will be at, or near to, the maximum potential. This varies from pump to pump, but an example being 2bar (20m-head pressure). This is referred to as deadhead or static pressure. As more water is allowed to flow from the terminal fitting, the pressure within the chamber falls accordingly. The flow and pressure that is maintained will depend on the design of the pumping chamber, speed of pump motor and restrictions within the supplies. Power-shower pumps usually deliver between 10 and 20ltr/min at running pressures between 1 and 3bar.

Plumbing Fault Diagnosis

For gravity-system and pumped-system plumbing fault diagnostics, common mistakes are:

- Connecting a mixer valve to gravity hot- and mains cold-water supplies, resulting in unbalanced pressures. (Always check product specification to ensure it is compatible with unbalanced supplies.)
- The cold supply needs to be taken from the bottom of the cold tank, at the opposite side from the mains inlet – taking the cold supply from the cistern directly beneath the float-operated valve is likely to draw air into the system because, as the cistern empties, air entering the cistern can be drawn into the supply to the mixer valve or the pump, causing erratic flow or air locks.
- Using quarter-turn service valves and stop-taps can restrict the supplies to the shower. On gravity systems, non-restrictive gate valves or full-way lever valves must be used.
- Taking the cold supply from the cold feed supplying the cylinder. This bad practice reduces the available amount of hot and cold water to the shower.
- Taking the hot supply from the expansion/vent pipe. This results in a total loss of flow to the shower when other outlets are in use and introduces air into a supply to a pump.
- Taking the hot supply pipe to the shower vertically from a tee-fitting located in the inclined section of pipe from the top of the cylinder. This results in air from the cylinder entering the supply to the shower. When fitting the tee at this position it must face downwards to allow air to pass by and escape via the expansion/vent pipe.
- Connecting to a cistern that has insufficient capacity and slow filling rate, whereby the cistern drains to the level of the take-off connection to the mixer/pump, resulting in air locks.
- Running pipes to the shower through the loft at a height that exceeds the water level in the cistern, resulting in a negative-head condition.
- Crossed supplies on the mixer, i.e. connecting hot water to the cold inlet of the mixer. Check whether the mixer can accommodate hot on the left and right.

The performance of a mixer shower can be compromised by incorrect plumbing connections.

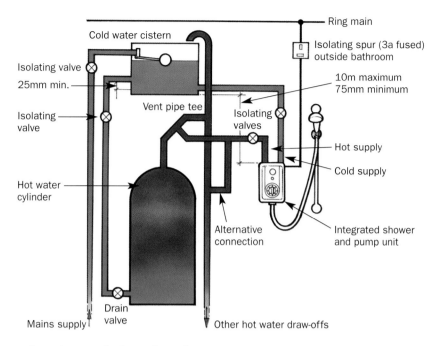

Plumbing diagram for an integrated mixer valve and pump.

Thermal Heatstore Units

Thermal heatstore units consist of a cylinder of hot water stored at low pressure, which is used to transfer heat into a flow of mains cold water as it passes through the unit. In their outward appearance, many resemble a gravity-fed system, consisting of either a separate cold-water cistern and hot-water cylinder or a combined cistern and cylinder. In these units, water in the cylinder is heated to between 60 and 65°C; this can be drawn off, as required, at the various hot taps within the property under gravity pressure.

The cylinder differs internally, where a coil of copper tube is wound within the hottest section of stored water. External cold in/hot out connections on the coil enable a dedicated water supply to a single mixer shower. Mains cold water is connected to the inlet. When the shower is operated, cold water flows through the coil, and is heated by the stored hot water; water to the shower is, therefore, delivered at mains pressure. The cold feed to the shower mixer is also taken from the cold mains supply.

Other higher output thermal store units exist, where the heated water in the cylinder is not drawn off at taps. In these units, the store of hot water is maintained at approximately 80°C. Domestic hot-water delivery to taps, showers, etc., is provided at mains pressure, as the heat transfer into the cold water takes place via the coil or plate heat-exchange process within the unit.

Suitable Shower Types for a Thermal Heatstore

Thermostatic mixer valves should be specified for units that are unable to maintain a constant hot-water temperature.

- Manual mixer valves.
- HP and GP thermostatic mixer valves.
- HP and GP bath mixer showers.
- Shower panels – high output thermal store units only.

Pressure compensating valves will operate satisfactorily on models incorporating a thermostatic blending valve on the outlet of the unit.

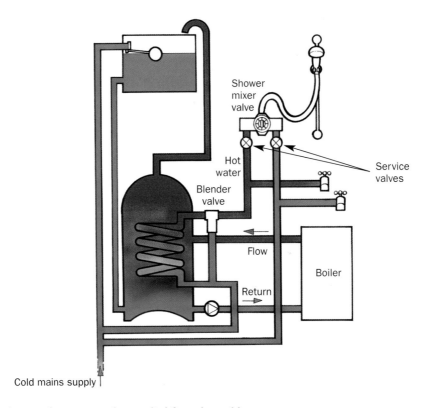

Plumbing diagram for a mixer valve supplied from thermal heatstore.

The primary factors that govern performance of showers fed by thermal heatstore units are:

- available temperature of stored hot water in the cylinder;
- heat-transfer characteristics of the coil or plate heat exchange inside the unit;
- ambient temperature of cold water entering the coil;
- number of outlets being supplied simultaneously (flow rate through the appliance).

With a number of variations on the principle, performance differs greatly from one make of thermal store to another; some having better heat-transfer characteristics than others. It should also be noted that when cold or hot water is being drawn off elsewhere, temperature and pressure fluctuations occur in the supplies to the shower. When operating at full poten-

tial, some thermal store units can provide powerful showers with pressures in excess of 1bar running pressure and flow rates ranging from 8 to 30ltr/min.

A pressure-reducing valve (PRV) is required if incoming mains water pressure exceeds the manufacturer's maximum specified running pressure. The PRV must be installed at a point in the cold supply where it provides a balanced pressure of both hot and cold water to the shower.

Unvented Hot-Water System

This system consists of a storage cylinder, which can be made from a variety of materials, e.g. copper, stainless steel or enamelled steel. A range of storage capacities is available for both domestic and commercial applications. Some units are similar in appearance to gravity-fed hot-water storage cylinders.

An unvented cylinder provides a known volume of stored hot water, usually at temperatures between

55 to 65°C. Water can be heated by an internal electric immersion heater, central heating indirect coil or by gas and oil burner direct flame.

The major difference between an unvented and gravity-fed cylinder, from a showering perspective, is the method of supplying cold water into the cylinder, an unvented cylinder is connected to the incoming mains cold-water supply at a higher pressure. A PRV is fitted in the cold supply to the cylinder to ensure that water pressure meets the level specified by the cylinder manufacturer. The maximum allowed pressure for any unvented cylinder being 3.5bar.

An unvented system is effectively a closed system, until such times as a terminal fitting (the mixer shower) is opened and hot water is released – as mains water pressure is forcing hot water out of the cylinder, a powerful shower can be achieved. Flow rates from 10 to 30ltr/min are the norm, although this will depend on the restrictions within the shower equipment; some mixer showers and showerheads are less restrictive than others.

> ## Suitable Shower Types for an Unvented System
>
> - Manual mixer valves.
> - HP and GP thermostatic mixer valves.
> - GP bath mixer showers.
> - Pressure compensating mixers.
> - Shower panels.

You need to be aware that pressure changes occur in the supplies to the shower when other terminal fittings are in use. Fluctuations can be minimized by taking the hot and cold supplies to the shower from specific areas on the system, i.e. the cold feed should be taken off directly after the PRV on the supply to the cylinder. If this is not possible, and the incoming cold-water supply pressure exceeds the specification on the shower, a separate PRV needs to be installed on the cold feed to the shower. This can be set to the same value as that fitted on the supply to the cylinder.

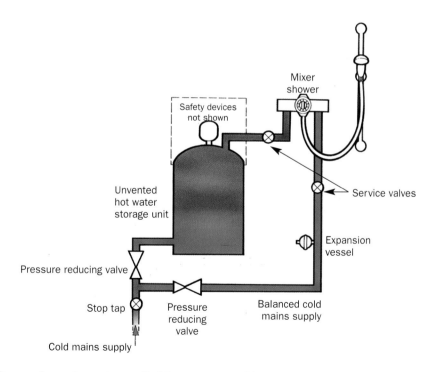

Plumbing diagram for a mixer valve supplied from an unvented hot-water system.

If the cold-water supply to a mixer shower is taken from a PRV containing a check valve, or there is a check valve elsewhere in the cold supply, which prevents thermal expansion returning back into the mains, then static pressure may exceed the specification of the shower. Installing a mini expansion vessel in the cold supply to the shower will prevent excessive pressure damaging the mixer valve.

Gas Combination Boilers – Multipoint Heaters

These hot-water appliances provide hot water on demand as and when required. Combination boilers cater for both central heating and domestic hot-water needs, whereas multipoint heaters provide domestic hot water only. Both types of appliance are available in a range of heating abilities. Sizes are quoted either in BTU (British Thermal Unit) ratings, e.g. 100,000 BTU/h output or kilowatt ratings.

Combination boilers and multipoints heat mains cold water instantaneously as it flows through a heat-exchange unit within the boiler.

Operating pressure for these units is usually

Information on Thermal Energy
1 BTU = 17.5 watt minutes, 100,000 BTU/H = 29kW.

between 0.5 to 10bar. Within this pressure range, sufficient water must flow through the boiler when a tap or shower is turned on to activate a flow sensor in the boiler. When activated, the flow sensor initiates heat transfer to the domestic hot-water circuit. The minimum flow to activate the water heating process is normally around 2 to 3ltr/min.

In terms of the shower, combi boilers and multipoint heaters are slightly more economical, as they only produce hot water on demand. The flow rate is dependant on the boiler rating and the ambient temperature of the incoming mains cold-water supply plus the hot-water temperature required at the mixer and a satisfactory mains pressure/flow for operation. Temperature and pressure fluctuations can occur when other outlets are operated.

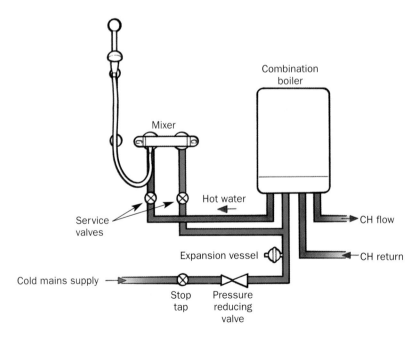

Plumbing diagram for a mixer valve supplied from combination boiler or multipoint heater.

Although hot water is available on demand, performance will vary throughout the year. A boiler can deliver (say) 12ltr/min in the height of summer, but in the depth of winter that can drop to around 7ltr/min.

As both hot and cold supplies to a shower mixer are from the mains supply, flow variations can occur when other outlets are opened. On very poor sites, this could result in a total loss of one or both supplies to the shower; satisfactory shower performance is therefore very reliant on good site conditions. The latest combi boilers, and some multipoint water heaters, are all of the modulating type. This means that, having set the hot-water temperature control on the boiler to a preferred temperature, e.g. 50°C, automatic adjustment (modulation) of the burner will occur, i.e. the gas flame will increase or decrease to maintain a relatively stable hot-water temperature. If a boiler is not of the fully modulating type, then water temperature will fluctuate when flow-rate adjustments occur at terminal fittings.

In the case of a thermostatic mixer valve, it will close off against an increasing hot-water temperature. This has the effect of water temperature in the boiler steadily increasing to a point where a

---

Suitable Shower Types for Use with Combi Boilers

- HP and GP thermostatic mixer valves.
- HP and GP bath mixer showers.
- Pressure-compensating mixers.
- Shower panels (high-output combination boilers only).

---

thermostat in the boiler switches off the gas burner completely. Water to the shower then runs cooler until the boiler thermostat resets and restarts the gas burner. This hot/cold cycling effect will be noticed at the shower.

You should be aware that combi boilers/multipoint heaters are not supplied with a PRV, therefore it may be necessary to install one into the cold supply if the mains pressure exceeds the maximum running pressure specified for the mixer.

It should be appreciated that when hot-water taps elsewhere in the house are turned on, while the shower is running, flow to the shower will decrease or even stop altogether. Where a check valve is fitted in the cold feed to the boiler, it may be necessary

---

Common Site Problems for Mixer Valves – Causes and Remedies

Most common problems that arise on mixer shower products can be resolved by conducting a few simple checks:

No water flowing.
- Has water been turned on fully at the isolating valves?
- Is the cold-water cistern at least 1m above the shower-head?
- Have inlet elbows/filters been checked for blockages?
- Is there an air-lock in the hot or cold supply?

Water too cold/cool.
- Is the domestic hot water hot enough? Check at taps for approx. 55–60ºC.
- Has the mixer been connected correctly to gravity hot and cold? If mains cold, re-plumb to cold-water cistern.

- Is the temperature acceptable by pressing the temperature over-ride button (increasing to a higher number)?

Water too hot.
- Is cold-water isolating valve fully open?
- Has cold inlet been checked for blockage?

Poor flow from shower-head.
- Has spray plate been de-scaled?
- Are isolating valves fully open?
- Have inlet filters, check valves, flow limiters been checked for any blockages?
- Is cold-water cistern a minimum of 1m above the shower-head?
- Is there an air-lock in the hot or cold supply?

to fit a mini expansion vessel to prevent static pressure increasing to a level that can damage the mixer valve. The flow sensor in the boiler must be capable of starting the heating process when a minimum of 3ltr/minute is flowing from a tap or shower valve.

General Installation Guidance

It is essential to flush out debris from the hot and cold supplies in order to prevent damage to the working parts of a mixer valve. Wherever possible this should be done prior to making final connections to the valve. If for any reason pipes cannot be flushed prior to making final connections, then a flushing cartridge may be supplied with the product. Failure to flush supplies can result in blocked filters or damage to valve components.

Particular attention must be given to ensuring installations are in accordance with water regulations/bye-laws and BS 6700 (specification for design, installation, testing and maintenance of services supplying water for domestic use within buildings and their curtilages).

SAFETY AND HEALTH – PRODUCT SAFEGUARDS

Things to check before buying or installing a shower control valve:

- All electric showers need to show that they are BEAB (British Electrotechnical Approvals Board) approved.
- Models need to have at least one safety device to prevent excessive temperatures. Most have a thermal cut-out (temperature sensing switch), which disconnects the heating elements if the outlet temperature exceeds a preset value.
- In addition, a flow or pressure sensor ensures that heating elements are turned off if the flow of water falls to below a minimum value, which would result in an excessive outlet temperature.
- Some form of pressure-relief device is also incorporated. Should abnormal pressure occur within the shower, e.g. due to a restriction in the showerhead, the device will relieve pressure safely to atmosphere.

CHAPTER 10

Frequently Asked Questions

FREQUENTLY ASKED QUESTIONS – BATHS

Q: Is the quality of acrylic baths as good as others?
A: Look for baths that meet BS 4305: Part 1/EN 198, so that their quality is guaranteed.

Q: What is the best way to clean an acrylic bath?
A: A soft cloth and soapy water is all that is needed to get a good finish. Rinse with clean water and wipe dry.

Q: Can I choose my bath from one supplier and the wash basin and toilet from other sources – will the colours match?
A: You can mix and match suppliers but the colours (even white) are not guaranteed to match – you would need to take responsibility for checking colour match.

Q: I like to soak in the bath, which bath keeps the water temperature warm for longest?
A: Acrylic baths have good insulation properties and keep the water warmer for longer – as does cast-resin.

Q: Which type of bath gives more choice of style?
A: No single type of bath gives a greater choice. If you are looking for roll-top or slipper bath, then cast-iron and cast-resin offer most choice. If standard baths, then acrylic and pressed steel have the widest range of shapes and sizes.

Q: My bathroom has limited space, what are the options for fitting a bath?
A: Several suppliers offer baths for smaller bathrooms. A standard bath is 1700mm long - check the Ideal Standard 'Space' range. They have a bath at 1200mm long and one at 1500mm that also includes a shower area.

Q: Are colours available in porcelain-enamel steel?
A: Yes, there is a good range of colours.

Q: Will my local domestic water supply stain my porcelain-enamel steel bath?
A: Whilst porcelain-enamel steel and acrylic baths are generally excellent in their ability to withstand water-soluble materials, cast-iron baths can be affected over time. Cleaning after use will help reduce any problems. Lemons left on a hard water stain will remove it.

Q: I want to change the position of my taps when I install a new bath, is that possible?
A: Yes, with the wide range of designs available taps can be located in various positions to suit any bathroom.

Q: I wish to install a bath with taps mounted on the wall, are baths available without tap holes?
A: Yes, most suppliers have baths in their range with no pre-cut tap holes.

Q: How do I make sure that I have a water-tight seal between the bath and the wall when it is installed?

A: Follow the instructions from the manufacturer. Importantly, use the wall brackets, if provided, to fix the bath to the wall. A silicone sealant can be used to make a neat seal. A good tip is to fill the bath with water before applying the sealant. Also available are sealing strips – one called 'Teleseal10' even allows adjustment for new-build installation where settlement can still be an issue.

Q: Is it better to fit the bath panels before or after the bathroom flooring is laid?

A: The panel needs to be fitted after the flooring is laid or it may need to be trimmed to make it easier to remove should there be any need for access. It is also simpler to get a neat finish if the panel is fitted on top of the flooring.

Q: Do baths come with a guarantee?

A: It varies between different suppliers. Some offer a 25-year guarantee.

Q: Do you need a special water supply to have a whirlpool bath?

A: No, whirlpool baths utilize standard hot and cold supplies found in all households.

Q: Are whirlpool baths noisy?

A: If installed correctly, they should work quietly and efficiently, but expect some noise.

Q: Do I need a big bathroom for a whirlpool bath?

A: No, they are available in a range of sizes. All the plumbing and the pump are usually hidden beneath the bath or within an airing cupboard, so they do not take up more space than a standard bath.

Q: Do whirlpool baths need specialist fitters?

A: Yes. They are best installed by professional plumbers/electricians.

FREQUENTLY ASKED QUESTIONS – SANITARYWARE

Q: Is all sanitaryware white?

A: All suppliers offer models in a variety of colours and finishes to complement any bathroom or washroom design. White is the most popular colour chosen today.

Q: Is all sanitaryware made from vitreous china?

A: WCs, washbasins and bidets have been traditionally made from vitreous china. Other materials, such as plastics, stainless steel, solid surface material, fireclay and fine fireclay, are used but very rarely. A few years ago glass washbasins were fashionable, but a lack of an overflow and difficulty in keeping them clean has seen their popularity wane. It was also difficult for designers to integrate the coloured glass into the rhythm of the overall bathroom design.

Q: What are the advantages of vitreous china?

A: It is the perfect finish for toilets and basins – it is extremely durable, easy to clean and can be in service for many years without any deterioration in performance and appearance.

Q: What are the advantages of wall-hung washbasins?

A: They bring a very modern and stylish look to the bathroom and by leaving the floor exposed beneath them, they help to make a room appear larger.

Q: Why do some washbasins have pedestals?

A: The larger the washbasin, the more support it will require. A pedestal provides the extra support and also conceals the trap, waste and fittings.

Q: When you fit a countertop basin does the water damage the top?

A: Granite, marble and corian are impervious, other materials will need adequate protection against water ingress. Laminate, for instance, will not be damaged by water, but if water can seep into the core to which the laminate is attached, then water it will cause damage. Sold timber needs an appropriate seal, which may need renewing annually.

Q: What is the difference between a low-level and a close-coupled WC?

A: Close-coupled is a more modern-looking toilet. With a 'close-coupled' the cistern is mounted and connected directly on to the back of the WC pan. A 'low-level' has the cistern mounted separately on the wall with a flush-pipe connecting into the back of the pan.

Q: Why would you use a 'back to wall' WC?

A: A 'back to wall' WC has the cistern concealed behind a false wall, which provides an easy to clean and very neat fitment, with only the cistern lever/pushbutton visible from the front. A back to the wall WC can also be fitted into bathroom furniture.

Q: Are toilet seats standard?

A: BS 1254 specifies requirements for toilet seats but not all seats on sale in the UK comply with the standard. There is a type of seat available for every type of WC. They can be either wooden or plastic and are available in a huge variety of colours, finishes and shapes.

Q: Are internal overflows mandatory?

A: No. A cistern can still be provided with an external overflow. Internal overflows are, however, more common in today's toilets.

Q: Do lever-operated siphons have internal overflows?

A: Some siphons do provide internal overflow. If the water level in a cistern rises above the required level, it will reach the 'spill-over' and cascade down the siphon down-leg and into the WC pan. Not all siphons provide this feature though.

Q: What are the WC flushing volumes?

A: UK WC flush volumes must not exceed 6ltr for new installations. There are many larger 7.5 and 9ltr-flush volumes still in use though.

Q: When installing low-level cisterns, is there a guide as to how high the cistern should be fixed?

A: There is no mandatory height for the cistern. It really is dependent on the bathroom dimensions available, such as the height of window sills and the maximum length of the flush-pipe provided with the cistern. It is a case of looking at the constraints of the particular application and taking a common sense approach – but the manufacturer's recommendations must be followed.

Q: Is there a standard outlet size for siphons and flush-valves?

A: Yes, as a general rule, siphons tend to have a standard (1½in) BSP outlet and flush-valves a standard (2in) BSP outlet. However, some products are available with adaptors.

Q: When fitting WCs into a new build application, is it necessary to flush the pipework through before finally completing the installation?

A: New pipework should always be flushed through. Many new cisterns contain compact 'Part 4'-type inlet valves that are fitted with a filter. If pipework is not flushed through properly, excess debris can clog the filter and prevent the valve from operating efficiently. This can lead to slow filling of the cistern.

Q: How do I determine which size siphon to fit into a cistern?

A: Simply measure internally from the cistern bottom to the 'invert' on the existing siphon (the point at which water travelling up the siphon body will spill down the down-leg).

Q: What type of inlet valve is most suitable for narrow, portrait-style cisterns?

A: 'Part 4'-inlet valves are perfect as, unlike the more traditional 'Part 3' models, they do not come with long float arms and large round floats. They are far more compact in size and will fit into the smaller sized cisterns.

Q: In dual-flush installations, what proportion of the full flush should the reduced flush represent?

A: The reduced flush volume should be no greater than two-thirds of the full flush volume. Therefore in a new 6ltr application, the reduced flush volume should not exceed 4ltr.

Q: Can a siphon be used in concealed cisterns fitted behind thick block walling?

A: Yes. Concealed lever kits are readily available to fit a wide range of concealed applications from 12mm-thick partitions up to concrete block walls, where the cistern is fixed to the rear wall. In this situation, the lever kit has to be long enough

121

to fit through the concrete block front wall and the duct in order to reach the cistern.

Q: Does a bidet have to be installed in a bathroom with a toilet?

A: Not necessarily. A bidet can be fitted on its own but they tend to be more commonly fitted alongside a WC.

Q: Can a squatting pan be fitted in any bathroom?

A: Theoretically yes, but the trap and bowl is largely beneath the top surface of the floor, so if they are installed on a solid floor, the floor will have to be dug out to accommodate. If fitted to a boarded floor, there needs to be enough depth beneath the boards for the bowl and trap.

FREQUENTLY ASKED QUESTIONS – SHOWER-TRAYS

Q: Should walls be tiled before fitting a shower-tray?

A: It has long been common practice on the Continent to seal the complete bathroom, which negates the concern for water escaping into the rest of the room during showering or bathing, This has led to the practice of tiling both the floor and the walls prior to installation of any bathroom equipment. In the UK, the practice is to control the water at the place of use, so we are careful that the shower-enclosure does not leak water on to the floor. So, in the UK, we tile the walls after installing a shower-tray to ensure a greater chance of a truly effective seal between the wall and the shower-tray.

Q: How high above the bathroom floor should a shower-tray be installed?

A: The simple answer is, it depends on many factors, such as: is the plumbing running above or below the bathroom floor? Is access to the trap required?

Q: When installing a shower-tray, how do I ensure that I can unblock the trap?

A: Shower-trays use less water than a bath and as a result the water flow rate through the waste trap is lower; this can cause a blockage in the trap. If possible, always make sure there is a moveable panel to access the trap for cleaning purposes. Alternatively, fit a top access waste that is designed to be removed from the inside of the shower-tray to facilitate cleaning.

Q: I want to install a ceramic shower-tray but my bathroom floor is uneven, what do I do?

A: Use a thin bed of silicone sealant or a weak sand and cement mixture (5:1) between the shower-tray and floor to level the floor.

Q: Do the patterns on shower-trays make them anti-slip?

A: Not unless the manufacturer specifically states this.

Q: How long are most shower-trays guaranteed for?

A: Depends on brand and material, and varies from supplier to supplier. To find out check in the brochure or ring the supplier's Customer Care Department. Alternately, visit the supplier's web-site.

Q: Should I buy a tray and shower-enclosure at the same time?

A: It is advisable to buy them together to ensure that they are compatible and of the same size.

Q: Do shower-trays move?

A: Not if installed correctly. It is important that the tray is installed to the manufacturer's instructions and the feet are securely screwed to the floor.

FREQUENTLY ASKED QUESTIONS – SHOWER-ENCLOSURES

Q: The opening between two walls is 830mm. What width of door do I need to purchase?

A: Telescopic profiles fitted on the frame achieve minimum and maximum figures. Check the width of the opening carefully at floor, waist and eye-level to determine the tolerances necessary. You can obtain advice from your supplier and also the manufacturer's brochure or web-site.

Q: There is an obstruction to the left of the opening of the shower-enclosure. Which type of door would be suitable?

A: Any obstruction makes it advisable to purchase an enclosure with a folding or sliding door, neither of which encroach on the outside of the enclosure door frame.

Q: I want to purchase a pumped shower and I am considering purchasing a bath-screen. Would this be sufficiently watertight for a powerful shower?

A: No – it is not advisable to use a pumped shower in conjunction with a single bath-screen due to the volume of water and spray.

Q: How do I install my product once I have purchased it?

A: The retailer may have their own in-house installation service, or should at least be able to recommend a professional tradesman who can install your product correctly. Many products come with easy to follow instructions should you wish to install the product yourself. Alternatively, some suppliers now provide a 'home installation service'.

Q: Can I install an enclosure into a defined space or shape?

A: Many suppliers offer a 'made-to-measure' service on some, though not all, of their enclosures and over-bath-screens. A variety of configurations can be tailor-made to suit your individual requirements with cut and angled glass and aluminium making up all sorts of unusual shapes and sizes. Such rooms will need to be tiled before measuring can take place.

Q: Can anyone help with the planning of my bathroom?

A: Provided that you buy your bathroom from them, many retailers offer a free design service, which can help plan your bathroom layout. Otherwise you could approach an architect or interior design company to help you.

Q: I have a small bathroom with limited space – are there space-saving shapes and designs?

A: Yes, a lot of suppliers offer compact-dimension showers, which will help if there is a problem on space and availability of access.

Q: Should I buy a tray and shower-enclosure at the same time?

A: It is advisable to buy them together to ensure that they are compatible and of the same size.

FREQUENTLY ASKED QUESTIONS – SHOWER VALVES

Q: How much flow can I expect to get from an electric shower?

A: The performance of all temperature-stabilized electric showers is governed by the following factors:

- kilowatt rating of the shower;
- water temperature entering the shower;
- voltage to the shower;
- preferred showering temperature.

At a showering temperature of 38°C, an electric shower will deliver 2.5–3.5ltr/min in winter increasing to 5–10ltr/min during the warmer months. The higher the kilowatts, the greater the flow of water for the desired temperature selected.

Q: Does a 10.5kW electric shower provide the same performance as a mixer-valve power-shower?

A: Typically a power-shower (a pump and mixer valve shower) or a mixer connected to a high-pressure hot-water system can provide flows of between 10 and 16ltr/min. During the summer months, when the cold-water supply temperature can reach 20°C, a 10.5kW electric shower can deliver 8–9ltr/min at 38°C. In winter, when ambient water temperature is cooler at around 5°C, performance will be less at 4–5ltr/min.

Q: What size cable can I use for my electric shower installation?

A: Cable size depends on a number of factors that will vary from one installation to another; such as, cable length, kW rating of the shower, cable routing and whether cable is in contact with thermal insulation or other cables. In all cases, cable selection must comply with the current IEE regulations. In order to know the actual cable size required, please contact a professional installer who is conversant with IEE regulations. As a guide only, the minimum size cable that can be used for units up to 8kW is 6mm. For higher rated units, it is strongly recommended to use a minimum of 10mm two-cable. Given there may be a requirement to upgrade to a higher rated unit in future, it is probably best to use a minimum of 10mm two-cable for all installations.

Q: Is it possible to connect an electric shower to a cold-water cistern and, if so, what head of water is required?

A: An electric shower can be fitted to a cold-water cistern providing the head of water is adequate. Typically, electric showers require between 0.7 and 1.5bar minimum operating pressure. 1m of head is equivalent to 0.1bar, therefore there must be 7–15m head, depending on the manufacturer's specifications. Head of water is measured from the base of the cold-water cistern to the shower-head. Some electric showers incorporate an integral pump. These units can be installed where the base of the cold-water cistern is as little as 75mm above the top of the unit. This is sufficient head to prime the pump the shower-head can in some cases be in a negative-head position.

Q: What is the minimum water pressure required for an electric shower designed to connect on to the mains cold supply?

A: Electric showers require a minimum operating pressure in order to activate switches controlling heating elements in the unit. A minimum flow at that pressure is also required for optimum temperature control and performance. Requirements differ for the wide range of showers on the market. Always check the manufacturer's specifications. Examples of pressure and flow requirements are:

- 8kW and 8.5kW showers – 1bar minimum running pressure at a minimum flow of 8ltr/min
- 9kW and 9.5kW showers – 1bar minimum running pressure at a minimum flow of 9ltr/min
- 10.5kW showers – 1.5bar minimum running pressure at a minimum flow of 11ltr/min.

In most cases, the mains cold-water supply will provide adequate pressure and flow. However, if the supply is unable to meet requirements, an electric shower can be connected to a cistern-fed pumped supply.

Q: Can a power-shower unit be fitted to the mains cold-water supply?

A: A power-shower unit contains a pump. The construction of the pump is such that it can only accept a low-pressure gravity (cistern-fed) supply. Connecting the shower to the mains will subject the pump to excess pressure and result in damage to the pump and leakage from the unit. Water regulations prohibit the connection of this type of pump to the mains water supply.

Q: Can an integral power-shower be installed on to a combi boiler?

A: All integral power-showers incorporate a pump and mixer valve, which can only be connected to low-pressure gravity supplies. Connecting to the high-pressure mains-fed combi boiler will damage the shower unit. This combination also contravenes the water regulations.

Q: I am fitting a shower panel and the hot supply is from a combi boiler. How can I be sure there will be enough flow from the combi to satisfy customer needs?

A: The performance of a combi boiler is determined by its kW rating and temperature can change dependent on season. The boiler-specification literature should provide flow-rate figures for a given temperature rise, enabling hot-water output throughout the year to be established. As a rough guide, each function on a shower panel, i.e. the overhead spray, hand-held spray and body jets, can each deliver from 8 to 14ltr/min, depending on supply pressure. To satisfy two functions simultaneously, effectively requires around 13ltr/min. If you are fitting a shower panel to gravity-fed water supplies, you will need to increase supply pressures by installing a twin impeller pump. Depending on the model of the shower panel and customer preferences, the pump should be rated at 1.5 to 4bar running pressure.

Q: How do you determine the pressure you will get to a shower-head when a mixer shower is connected to gravity supply?

A: The principle is that for every 1m-head of water (as measured from the base of the cold-water cistern to the top of the shower-head), there will be a pressure in the shower-head of 0.1bar. This is a theoretical pressure, as restrictions within pipe-fittings and the shower mixer valve will reduce the pressure to a degree. Providing only minimal restrictions are present in the supplies and terminal fitting, the additional measurement (height) of water within the cistern will usually compensate for pressure losses in the supplies. It can be seen that a shower requiring 1bar minimum operating pressure, would need to be connected to a cistern located 10m above the shower-head.

Q: Is it acceptable to install two power-showers on to a 115ltr (25 gallon) cold-water cistern if they are going to be used simultaneously?

A: When two power-showers are in operation simultaneously they can draw around 30ltr (6 gallons) per minute from the cold-water cistern. If the cold water entering the cistern through the float-operated valve is less than this amount, then the level of water in the cistern may fall to the level of the connections to the showers. Air will then be drawn into the supplies, adversely affecting shower performance and potentially damaging the pumps. It is advisable to increase the cistern capacity to at least 230ltr (50 gallons) and check that the fill rate of the cistern is adequate to cater for all outlets that are likely to be in use simultaneously.

Q: Can I fit an all-in-one power-shower in a loft-conversion bathroom?

A: All-in-one power-showers must be installed below the level of the cold-water cistern. In a loft conversion, it is unlikely that the cistern can be raised above the shower unit. If a pumped shower is required, it is necessary to install a twin impeller pump with some form of negative-head switching and a surface-mounted or built-in mixer shower. The pump must be sited below the level of the water in the cistern, but with negative-head switching, the hot and cold supply from the pump can rise vertically to the shower sited above the level of water in the cistern.

Q: Do I need to use a cylinder flange when installing a mixer or power-shower?

A: Most leading shower suppliers agree it is not necessary to use cylinder flanges when installing a single domestic power-shower. Teeing into the inclined section of pipe from the top of the cylinder is the preferred method of connection. Providing the tee is pointing down, air released from the heated water in the cylinder will bypass the tee and escape out of the expansion pipe. If it is not possible to fit the tee in this fashion, it can be installed in the falling supply to other outlets, providing it is below the expansion pipe tee and is the first take off point before other taps.

Q: Can a mixer valve be installed to unbalanced supplies of mains-fed cold water and gravity-fed hot water?

A: Water regulations permit the connection of mixer taps and shower mixer valves to mains-fed cold water and gravity-fed hot water, providing there is a check valve in both supplies to prevent cross-flow. Check with the manufacturer's installation instructions that the product can be used to mix mains and gravity supplies.

Q: I have a thermal store hot-water system in my property. How many mixer showers can be fed from one of these appliances?

A: The output from a thermal store unit depends on its size (stored volume), heat transfer capability and the water pressure entering the unit. Some are only capable of delivering sufficient hot water to one mixer shower, whereas others can supply three or four showers simultaneously. Always check, before selecting any shower, that the capacity of the heating appliance is compatible with the shower and required usage.

Q: I have fitted a thermostatic mixer shower to a combi boiler system only to find the shower temperature is fluctuating, I thought a thermostatic mixer was supposed to remain at a constant temperature.

A: The most common reason for this symptom is when the combi-boiler is not fully modulating (i.e. the gas flame is not regulated in sympathy with the flow of water through the heat exchange unit) and is therefore not maintaining stable hot-water temperature to the shower. As hot water entering the shower increases in temperature a thermostatic mechanism will adjust to restrict hot water entering the valve. In turn, flow through the boiler is reduced and the temperature reaches a point where a thermostat switches off the burner. Water temperature will then reduce before the thermostat resets, this will results in the shower constantly cycling between hot and cool.

Q: The flow from my mixer shower is less than I expected. What is the usual performance of a shower on a gravity system?

A: Flow-rate from mixer showers varies depending on the available head of water and restrictions within the supply and valve. To ensure optimum performance from gravity-fed mixer showers, the following guidance should be followed:

- use as few 90 degree elbows as possible and, where possible, use pulled bends;
- use full way lever or gate valves, do not fit restrictive stop taps or quarter-turn service valves;
- follow manufacturer's recommendations regarding pipe size;
- ensure the mixer is specified for low-pressure application;
- always flush out pipes before connecting on to avoid debris blocking inlet filters.

Q: My thermostatic mixer shower is supplied from a combi boiler and I cannot achieve a hot enough showering temperature. What could the problem be?

A: The most common causes of this symptom are:

- The flow of water through the shower is too great and the boiler is unable to heat the water to the required temperature. Isolating the cold supply and measuring the hot-water flow and temperature through the mixer on its maximum hot setting should establish whether this is the case. If so, it will be necessary to fit some form of flow-limiting device on the inlet or outlet of the shower.
- A blockage has occurred in the hot supply thereby limiting the amount of hot water available to mix with the cold. Turning the temperature control on the shower to fully hot then fully cold should provide an indication of whether the hot and cold supply entering the mixer are of equal volume.

Q: I am looking to install a mixer shower on to a thermal store hot-water system. Can I fit a pressure-compensating mixer shower to this type of system?

A: Pressure-compensating valves can be specified for this type of high-pressure system. A pressure-compensating mixer shower is designed to maintain the set showering temperature when a pressure change occurs in either the hot or cold supply, i.e. when another tap is turned on in the property. However, this type of mixer shower does not respond to any changes that occur in the hot-water supply temperature. Providing the thermal store unit is capable of maintaining a constant water temperature when other taps are operated, then a pressure-compensating valve can maintain comfortable showering temperature. Where there are noticeable fluctuations in thermal-store domestic hot-water temperature, then a thermostatic mixer valve should be specified.

FREQUENTLY ASKED QUESTIONS – BRASSWARE

Q: What do you do if a tap/mixer leaks?

A: Isolate the water supplies. Remove the tap head-work (usually by removing the 'indice cap' and removing the screw underneath, or loosening a grub screw, which will allow the handle to be pulled off). Clean the seating, if the tap has rubber washers, and check the sealing washer and any O-rings are in good condition, replacing as necessary. Replace the cartridge if there is any doubt about the condition of any ceramic discs.

Q: Why does my basin-waste leak?

A: First, check the silicone seal between the waste flange and the basin (it may appear as if it is the plug cannot hold water, but the water may be actually seeping under the waste flange into the slots on the waste underneath). If this appears to be in good working order, check that the plug and waste are not damaged.

Q: Has my tap/mixer got ceramic discs or standard elastomeric (rubber) washers?

A: If the operation of the tap is based on small amounts of rotation (quarter or half-turn) from fully off to fully on, then the tap is likely to be ceramic-disc operation. However, the only true way to identify this is by removing it and checking visually. The presence of two ceramic discs in a cartridge, rather than a rubber sealing washer, provides confirmation.

Q: What are the benefits of ceramic discs over conventional sealing washers?

A: Ceramic discs have higher resistance to corrosion and wear, and thus require less maintenance. They are also much easier to operate, so are of benefit to the elderly and the less able.

Q: Is it possible to change the handle and headwork? How do you remove them?

A: Yes, providing they are compatible. This is possible usually by removing the 'indice cap' and removing the screw underneath, or loosening a grub screw, which will allow the handle to be pulled off. The headwork or ceramic disc cartridge can then be removed.

Q: What is dual flow or single flow?

A: The terms dual or single flow apply to mixer-tap spouts: A 'dual flow' spout is split internally by a 'wall' into two separate 'channels' or tubes to keep the flow of the hot and cold water separate, to the point of discharge. A 'single flow' spout requires the hot and cold water to mix within the body of the tap.

Q: Why is it important to ensure that high-pressure taps are not used on a low-pressure system?

A: If a tap requires high pressure it will not perform adequately on a low-pressure system. Therefore, the flow from the tap will be less than satisfactory. Usually the waterways in the fitting are much smaller in a high-pressure tap, so when installing it on a low-pressure system, you will frequently see a much reduced flow of water out of the tap, invariably one that is not fit for the purpose you require.

Q: What is the recommended way to clean taps?

A: All surface finishes will wear if not cleaned correctly. The only safe way to clean your tap/mixer is to wipe with a soft damp cloth. Stains can be removed using washing-up liquid. All bath cleaning powders and liquids, even the non-scratch cleaners, are likely to damage the surface of the fitting. Do not use bleach. Wiping after use will avoid the formation of scale caused by hard water drying on the surface. The build-up of soap deposits and lime-scale can prove difficult to remove and should be avoided.

Q: What is the recommended way to clean gold-plated taps?

A: Harsh abrasives and general bathroom cleaners are not recommended. Gold finishes are softer than chrome plate and special care must be taken when cleaning. Use only diluted liquid soap. Clean regularly, rinse and wipe dry.

Q: How do you remove lime-scale build up on taps?

A: Rather than using an aggressive cleanser, the safest way to remove lime-scale is with a natural citric acid, e.g. lemon juice or vinegar. Rinse afterwards and wipe dry.

Q: What guarantee will I get?

A: Most taps come with a minimum guarantee; which can vary from different suppliers from one year to ten years. However, in most cases this only covers manufacturing or material defects, and will not cover your need to replace seals or washers, as this is dependent on usage and water-supply conditions, e.g. debris in water or excessive lime-scaling.

Industry Standards

BATHS

BS 4305: Part 1–EN 198: 1987.
Specification for finished baths. General requirements, functional and physical characteristics to give satisfactory performance, and tests. National appendices give advice on labelling and information.

BS 1390: 1990.
Specification for baths made from vitreous enamelled sheet steel.

BS 1189: 1986.
Specification for baths made from porcelain-enamelled cast-iron.

BS EN 60335–2–60: 1998.
Whirlpool baths – For baths for indoor use, including equipment for circulating air or water to baths. To be read in conjunction with BS EN 60335–1: 1995. Replaces BS EN 60335–2–60: 1991 which remains current.

SANITARYWARE

BS 1212–3: 1990.
Specification for diaphragm-type float-operated valves (plastic bodied) for cold-water services only (excluding floats).

BS 1212–4: 1991.
Specification for compact-type float-operated valves for WC flushing cisterns (including floats).

BS 1254: 1981 (2000).
Specification for WC seats (plastics).

BS 3402: 1969.
Quality of vitreous china sanitaryware.

BS 5627: 1984.
Specification for the plastic connectors for use with horizontal outlet vitreous china WC pans.

BS 6465 Part–1: 1994.
Code of practice for scale of provision, selection and installation of sanitary appliances.

BS 6465 Part–2: 1996.
Code of practice for space requirements for sanitary appliances.

BS EN Publications

BS EN 31: 1999.
Pedestal washbasins. Connecting dimensions.

BS EN 32: 1999.
Wall-hung washbasins. Connecting dimensions.

BS EN 33: 1999.
Pedestal WC pans with close-coupled flushing cistern. Connecting dimensions.

BS EN 34: 1992.
Specification for wall-hung WC pan. Wall-hung WC pan with close-coupled cistern. Connecting dimensions.

BS EN 35: 2000.
Bidets with over-rim supply. Connecting dimensions.

BS EN 36: 1999.
Wall Hung Bidets with over-rim supply. Connecting dimensions.

BS EN 37: 1999.
WC pans with independent water-supply. Connecting dimensions.

BS EN 38: 1992.
Specification for wall-hung WC with independent water-supply. Connecting dimensions.

BS EN 997: 1999.
WC pans with integral trap.

TAPS AND MIXERS

BS 5412:1996.
Specification for low-resistance single taps and combination tap assemblies (nominal size ½ and ¾in) suitable for operation at PN 10 max, and a minimum flow pressure of 0.01MPa (0.1bar). The standard specifies the dimensional, water-tightness, pressure-resistance, hydraulic, mechanical strength and endurance characteristics with which size ½ and ¾in single taps and combination taps shall comply. Replaces Parts 1 to 5 of the dual-numbered BS 5412 and BS 5413.

BS 1010.
Specification for draw-off taps and stop-valves for water services (screw-down pattern).

BS EN 1111: 1999.
Sanitary tapware. Thermostatic mixing valves (PN10). General technical specification for use in bathrooms and kitchens.

BS EN 1287: 1999.
Sanitary tapware. Low-pressure mechanical mixing valves. General technical specification. Replaces BS 1415–1: 1976.

BS 7942: 2000.
Performance and material requirements, including test methods. Three distinct types of thermostatic mixing valves for use in care establishments.

BS 6700: 1997.
Specification for design, installation, testing and maintenance of services supplying water for domestic use within buildings and their curtilages. Combines requirements and recommendations for systems for pipes, fittings and connected appliances installed to supply buildings with water for drinking and other purposes. To be read in conjunction with CP 342–2: 1974.

BS EN 200: 1992.
Sanitary tap. General technical specifications for single taps and mixer taps (nominal size ½in) PN 10. Minimum flow pressure of 0.05MPa (0.5bar) Dimensional, water-tightness, pressure-resistance, hydraulic, mechanical strength, mechanical endurance and acoustic characteristics with which the single taps and mixer taps shall comply.

BS 5775: 1993 (2001) Parts 0–15.
Specification for quantities, units and symbols.

BS EN 12540: 2000.
Corrosion protection of metals. Electro-deposited coatings of nickel plated. Specification for electroplated coatings of nickel and chromium.

EN 200.
General specification for single taps and mixer taps (nominal size ½in) PN10. Minimum flow pressure – 0.5 bar.

SHOWER-ENCLOSURES

EN 14428: 2004 (E).
Shower-enclosures – functional requirements and test methods. This European standard document has the status of British Standard. It specifies requirements for shower-enclosures for domestic purposes, which ensure that the product, when installed in accordance with the manufacturer's installation instructions, gives satisfactory performance when used as intended. (For the purposes of this document the term 'domestic purposes' includes use in hotels, accommodation for students, hospitals and similar buildings, except when special medical provisions are required.)

The following referenced documents are indispensable for the application of this document. For dated references, only the edition cited applies. For undated references, the latest addition of the referenced document (including any amendments) applies.

BS 6700.
Specification for design, installation, testing and maintenance of services supplying water for domestic use within buildings and their cartilages.

EN 12150–1:2000.
Glass in building – thermally toughened soda lime silicate safety glass – Part 1: definition and description.

EN ISO 2409.
Paints and varnishes – cross-cut test (ISO 2409:1992).

ISO 7599.
Anodizing of aluminium and its alloys. General specifications for anodic oxide coatings on aluminium.

ISO 7892.
1988, Vertical building elements – Impact resistance test – Impact bodies and general test procedures.

BS 6206: 1981 (1984).
Specification for impact performance requirements for flat safety glass and safety plastics for use in buildings.

SHOWER-TRAYS

BS EN 251: 1992.
Shower-trays Connecting Dimensions. Connecting dimensions for Shower-trays regardless of materials. Supersedes any previous Standards relating to Shower-trays.

SHOWER VALVES

BS 7671 – otherwise referred to as IEE 16th Edition Wiring Regulations.
The IEE prepares regulations for the safety of electrical installations for buildings, the IEE Wiring Regulations (BS 7671) now having become the standard for the UK and many other countries.
www.iee.org/Publish/WireRegs/about-bs7671.cfm.

BS 3036.
Semi-enclosed (rewirable) fuse/BS 88–HBC fuses. The devices used to detect such overloads, and to break the circuit for protection against them, fall into three main categories:

1. Semi-enclosed (rewirable) fuses to BS 3036 and cartridge fuses for use in plugs to BS 1362.
2. High-breaking capacity (HBC) fuses to BS 88 and BS 1361. These fuses are still often known as high-rupturing capacity (HRC) types.
3. Circuit breakers, miniature and moulded case types to BS EN 60898.

BS 6700.
Specification for design, installation, testing and maintenance of services supplying water for domestic use within buildings and their cartilages.
www.iphe.org.uk/consumer/techfaq.html.

BS EN 1111 (HP).
Specification for high-pressure TMV type 2 mixer valves.

BS EN 1287 (LP).
Specification for low-pressure mixing valves.

WRC Ltd–Water Research Centre Ltd.
WRC Ltd provides analysis, testing and consultancy in the areas of public and environmental health by combining strong laboratory capabilities with expert interpretation. WRC–NSF is a joint venture of WRC plc and NSF International with laboratories in South Wales and the Thames Valley.
http://www.wrcnsf.com.
(References to water regulations apply to England and Wales. Data may vary for Scotland and Northern Ireland – please check for specific regulations applicable.)

Water (Water Fittings) Regulations 1999.
The Water Fittings Regulations (or Byelaws 2000 in Scotland) are national requirements for the design, installation and maintenance of plumbing systems, water fittings and water-using appliances. Their purpose is to prevent misuse, waste, undue consumption or erroneous measurement of water and to prevent contamination of drinking water. They replace the former Water Supply Byelaws, which each water supplier has administered for similar purposes for many years.
www.wras.co.uk/regulations/default.asp.

Water Bylaws.

The Water Fittings Regulations, replace water bylaws (in governing the prevention of waste, misuse, undue consumption, contamination and erroneous measurement of public water supplies in domestic and commercial plumbing installations) and represent important protection for public health and the environment.

The regulations are based on performance standards, e.g. British Standards or those European Standards being mandated under the Construction Products Directive. www.legislation.hmso.gov.uk/stat.thm.

IEE Wiring Regulations.

The IEE manages the national committee JPEL/64, which prepares and updates the regulations for the safety of electrical installations in buildings, and publishes the standard BS 7671:2001 (the IEE Wiring Regulations). It also provides and publishes extensive guidance upon the standard as well as related codes of practice. http://www.iee.org/Publish/WireRegs/index.cfm.

Building Regulations.

The building regulations are a set of minimum requirements designed to secure the health, safety and welfare of people in and around buildings and to conserve fuel and energy in England and Wales. They are made by the Secretary of State under powers given by Section 1 of The Building Act 1984.

www.odpm.gov.uk/stellent/groups/odpm_buildreg/documents/sectionhomepage/odpm_buildreg_page.hcsp.

Local Building Control Office.

Building control is an umbrella term covering all Local Authority Building Control Departments in England and Wales. These departments have a statutory duty to enforce building regulations. The building regulations are designed to ensure the highest standards of construction apply to all buildings, and that the health and safety of people using and working in and around buildings is adequately provided for. www.labc-services.co.uk.

Part P of the Building Regulations.

Part P, brings domestic electrical installation work in England and Wales under the legal framework of the building regulations. It will, for the first time, place a legal requirement for safety upon electrical installation work in dwellings, although the sector is highly regarded for its high levels of conformity with its chief standard, BS 7671. www.iee.org/Publish/WireRegs/PartP.cfm.

British Electromechanical Approvals Board (BEAB).

These regulations relate to the BEAB product certification schemes and the use of Marks licensed by BEAB. www.beab.co.uk.

Glossary

Acrylic A chemical compound which is used in the form of a flat sheet that is vacuum-moulded into the shape of a bath. Light, warm and easy to maintain – acrylic is strengthened using baseboards and GRP.

Acrylic-capped stone resin Polyester stone and resin liquid that is poured into a mould to produce an extremely strong, low-level shower-tray – usually with an acrylic surface.

Adjustable feet Devices incorporating a mechanical adjustment facility that supports the bath. They accommodate unevenness in the floor and usually provide adjustment of the rim height within a limited range.

Adjustable legs Devices that support shower-trays and offer a mechanical adjustment facility, which accommodates unevenness in the floor.

Adjustable swivel unions Offset connection pieces that can be swivelled to suit differing centres of the supply pipes before tightening.

Air switch A manual means of over-riding a flow switch for initial energizing of the pump.

Air-lock A pocket of air that has been trapped within the water-pipe, restricting or halting the flow of water through the pipe.

All-in-one power-showers A shower control comprising a housing that carries a pump and an integrated shower control. It needs a low pressure, and a cistern fed supply of stored hot and cold water.

Angled flow Water discharges from the tap at an angle, rather than vertically downwards. Useful to ensure water discharges well into a bowl when hand-washing is intended.

Anti-surge A feature that restricts the possibility of fluctuating volumes of water movement through the system.

Anti-entrapment device When the water-suction inlet is covered, the system cuts out.

Anti-rotation washer Washer fitted between a tap and an appliance, to prevent the tap from turning during use.

Ascending spray The adjustable water outlet found in the bowl of some bidets.

Automatic air vent A mechanical device similar to a car carburettor float-chamber that is used to remove quantities of air entrapped in plumbing pipework.

BEAB British Electrotechnical Approvals Board.

Back nuts Nuts used under an appliance to tighten and hold a tap in place.

Back-siphoning or back-flow Syphonic action causing the air-gap to be bridged between the clean mains water, either in the mains supply or after it has been stored, and used (grey) water from the shower-tray, toilet bowl, bidet or even the bath. The grey water may be carrying bacteria or material that will encourage the growth of bacteria and contaminate the clean water supply to the house, or even to the neighbourhood.

Back to wall WC WC with integral sides to conceal the trap. Usually used with a cistern hidden behind the wall, panelling ot fitted furniture.

Ball float A ball-operated valve used to control the inlet of water into a cistern.

Bar A unit of measurement of water pressure approximately equivalent to a column of water 10m high or 14.5lbf/in (or 100 kPa) per bar.

Bar (pressure) A unit of measurement of water supply pressure approximately equivalent to a column of water 10m high.

Basin mixer Water fitting (tap) on a washbasin that usually mixes hot and cold water within the body of the fitting.

Basin taps Taps of pillar-type construction. Available in hot or cold types.

Bath and shower mixer A single body fitting, requiring two tap holes for hot and cold water supplies, which mixes water within the body of the fitting. A diverter can channel water to either a spout to fill the bath or to a shower outlet via an attached flexible hose.

Bath filler Similar to basin mixers, but with a larger valve and higher flow levels, suitable for filling baths.

Bath panel Covers usually made from plastic, to conceal the underside of a bath and the connecting pipework.

Bath taps A pair of pillar taps with larger valves and higher flow levels making them suitable for the larger volumes of water needed to fill a bath within a reasonably short time.

Bidet A bidet is essentially a low-height washbasin, designed for washing the genitory-urinary area without the need for bathing or showering.

Bi-fold door A bi-fold door 'concertinas' when opening to give the space to enter or leave a shower-enclosure. Used where space is at a premium. It can be used on its own in a recess or in conjunction with side or in-fill panels to make a variety of shapes for shower-enclosures.

Body jets Wall-mounted shower sprays usually installed in multiples.

Bonding clamp A metal strap fastened to a pipe or fitting to enable electrical bonding (earthing).

Bottle trap Compact trap containing a water-seal to prevent foul air from drains entering a room.

Box spanner A simple socket spanner with a hollow centre that fits over a threaded inlet tail to tighten/un-tighten a nut.

Built-in Referring to a shower valve, describes one that is installed with the body of the valve recessed into the wall.

Bulkhead fitting *See* Wall Outlet Connector.

Cast-iron Iron poured (or cast) to a mould to form the shape of a bath. Very strong and rigid but heavy and cold. Surface is coated with porcelain-enamel to provide attractive, easy clean finish.

Centrifugal A type of pump, which draws water in through the eye or centre of the impeller, forcing it out to the external edges of the pump by centrifugal force. Water is then discharged vertically.

Ceramic disc valve A type of tap control valve where the functional parts are ceramic discs with V-shaped openings that are used to open and close water flow – when the openings line up, the water flows; when they do not align, the water is shut off. Sometimes referred to as quarter-turn taps, because it only takes a quarter turn from full on to off.

Ceramic discs Hard-wearing ceramic discs create a positive on/off control unless ports are aligned. Popular due to low maintenance and easy quarter or half-turn operation.

Check valves An in-line valve connected into the water supply pipe, which allows water to flow in only one direction. In some cases a check valve is required by water regulations to prevent back-flow.

Chrome plating Coating on tap bodies to enhance aesthetics.

Cistern A container housing the flushing mechanism and flushing water for a WC. It is normally fitted with a float-operated valve and an overflow warning pipe.

Clamping plate An alternative to back nuts. Mainly used on monobloc taps to hold the tap in place.

Claw spanner Tool for unscrewing or tightening nuts that secure water-fittings. Clamping jaws are usually serrated for extra grip (protect any decorative finishes before use,) which tighten to prevent slip – depending on the directions of use.

Closed-coupled WC WC cistern is mounted on the top plate of a WC pan.

Concealed bracket A bracket that is obscured from view and is used for attaching wall-hung washbasins to the wall.

Cold-water storage cistern Fixed container for holding water at atmospheric pressure, usually used for providing a feed to a vented domestic hot-water cylinder. It can also be used to provide a vented cold supply to terminal fittings.

Combination boiler Boiler that heats water as used. Fed by the mains, hot and cold water are balanced when supplying fittings. Does not require a hot-water cylinder or cold-water tank. Also heats water for central heating system.

Combination systems Whirlpool and spa systems combined into one bath.

Compression fitting A nut and 'olive' that compresses around copper pipes when tightened to create a water tight seal.

Concealed cistern A cistern that is fitted behind a (false) wall so that only the operating mechanism can be seen.

Conventional baseboard Usually made of chipboard. Bonded to the bottom of a bath to provide support and rigidity.

Corner bath Bath designed to fit into the corner of a bathroom, with the bathing area positioned diagonally across the corner.

Countertop basin A washbasin fitted into a worktop surface from above.

Countertop basin (under countertop) A basin that fits beneath the countertop and is held in position with the aid of clips and/or brackets.

Cradle Metal support arrangement for baths that usually accommodate adjustable feet for supporting a bath above the floor.

Cross-flow The water flow from one side of a hot/cold water mixer to the other, possibly leading to a contamination of the water supply.

Cylinder flange A plumbing fitting that can be fitted to a hot-water cylinder to provide a dedicated hot-water supply to a terminal fitting.

Deck mounted Fitting required to be installed on to a horizontal surface.

Distributing pipe Means any pipe (other than a flush-pipe or warning pipe) conveying water from a cold-water storage cistern.

Diverter A fitting used to control the direction of water to various outlets.

Double check valve (verifiable) A device that is designed to prevent back-siphoning, consisting of two check valves in series with a test point between the two.

Double-end bath Bath designed for use by two people, usually with provision for taps to be fixed along one of the sides.

Double pole switch An electrical switching device in which the continuity of both the mains live and neutral is broken upon the action of the switch, giving a contact separation of at least 3mm. The earth always remains connected.

Dual-flushing cistern A flushing cistern that provides discharges of two different volumes, the selection being made by the user.

Duty cycle Rating as specified on the pump product. The operating time of a pump expressed as a time 'on' and a time 'off'. A continuously rated pump can be operated non stop.

Dynamic pressure/maintained pressure The water pressure in the pipework to a fitting whilst flow is taking place.

ELCB Earth leakage circuit breaker.

Electroplated Common method of applying a tough metal coating, e.g. nickel/chrome to a brass product.

Enamelled A method of applying a glass finish to a metal product, e.g. bath.

Element or **electric element** The electrical element, which heats the water in an electric shower.

Encapsulated baseboard Usually made of chipboard bonded to the bottom of a bath to provide support and rigidity but also completely 'sealed in' by the reinforcing material.

Equamatic A term used to describe a pressure-balancing mixing valve.

Equilibrium float valve A compact size type of float valve operated by the small float and pressure of water.

Fibre washer A washer made from a tough fibrous material used as an alternative to rubber.

Fireclay A ceramic product used for larger sanitaryware items. A more dense mix of vitreous china, used in larger ceramic pieces such as Belfast sinks and shower-trays.

Fixed shower-head A fixed height shower-head, which cannot be moved.

Flange The 'collar' usually found around the base of a tap.

Flexible hose Pipe made from flexible material, sometimes protected by a metal outer cover. Used commonly to transfer water from the shower valve to the shower-head spray.

Float-operated valve Is a valve used to control the flow of water into a cistern, the valve being controlled by the level of water in the cistern.

Float valve Inlet valve found inside a cistern, which control the in-flow of water often using a ball type float.

Flow The volume of water moving through the pipes or from the tap or shower-head. It can expressed in ltr/min, gallons/h or m^3.

Flow pressure *See* Dynamic Pressure.

Flow rate Speed at which water flows, e.g. through a fitting. Usually measured in ltr/s or ltr/min.

Flow regulator A device with moving parts that responds to variable inlet pressures to control flow at a reasonably constant rate. These are subdivided into two types: (a) fixed – manufactured in a range of pre-determined flow-rate settings; (b) variable – manually adjustable to provide different flow rate settings.

Flow restrictor A device with no moving parts that restricts flow. Unlike a flow regulator it does not keep a constant flow when the supply pressure varies.

Flow switch Electromechanical device that senses a gravity flow of water, which is typically used to start a pump.

Flush-pipe A pipe that connects low- or high-level cisterns to a WC pan.

Flushing cistern Cistern fitted with a device, operated automatically or by the user, that discharges water to cleanse a WC pan, urinal or slop hopper.

Flushing valve Mechanical device used to clear the water out of the cistern on a toilet. Relatively new in the UK, valves are operated by a pushbutton or electronic sensor. Flushing takes place when a seal over the outlet hole is lifted, allowing the water in the cistern to be evacuated into the WC pan, where its flush action clears the contents into the soil pipe.

Frameless over-bath screens A screen of glass to enclose the water room from a shower-head fitted to a bath. Frameless refers to the fact that it has no metal frame into which the glass fits.

Fused spur A branch off an electrical ring main to a double pole switched connection box fitted with a fuse to enable the connection of a fixed electrical appliance.

Glass reinforced plastic (GRP) Reinforcing material comprising strands of glass fibre and high quality resin (sometimes known as glass reinforced polyester).

Glaze A glass-like coating applied as a spray to vitreous china or fireclay, fired in a kiln during the manufacturing process to give a hard-wearing, non-porous coating.

Grub screw Small headless screw used for locating or locking parts together.

Hand shower A shower-head attached to a flexible shower hose, also termed a shower handset.

Hand-rinse basin Wall-hung basin that has an overall width of 500mm or less and usually stands out less from the wall.

Handset *See* Hand Shower.

Handset Holder *See* Riser.

Hand-wheel and lever Means of providing connection to the headwork to facilitate easy manual control of on/off and flow through taps.

Header tank *See* Cold Water Storage Cistern.

High-level WC The WC cistern is mounted on the wall usually around head-height, connected to the WC pan by a long flush-pipe.

High pressure Water pressure usually higher than 1 or 2bar.

Horizontal rod Component of a pop-up waste connecting to the vertical controlling rod.

Hinged swing door Hinged doors may or may not require a frame but the door is a pure safety-glass panel of between 5 and 10mm thick. Hinged doors are ideal to fit across an alcove or in a corner with a matching side-panel.

Horizontal outlet The outlet of the pan comes straight out horizontally at the back of the WC.

Hose restrainer A device through which a shower hose passes to restrict its reach into other water-carrying fixtures and thus prevent the chances of back-siphoning.

Hose retaining ring Same as a hose restrainer.

Hot-water cylinder Means a cylindrical closed vessel capable of containing hot water under pressure greater than atmospheric.

IEE Institute of Electrical Engineers.

Impeller The internal part of the pump that is driven by the motor, and is used to pressurize the water.

Indirect cylinder A hot-water cylinder in which the stored water is heated by a primary heater through which hot water is circulated from a boiler. There is no mixing of the primary and secondary water.

Inlet socket Recessed hole in a WC pan for connection of a flush-pipe.

Inlet tails Means for providing connection to the hot and cold water supplies. Either rigid (plain or threaded) or flexible.

Instant showers The instant electric or gas showers heat water directly from the mains to give hot water on demand – ideal for frequent use. They are economical to buy and to run but they do not give the flow rate of a mixer shower or a pumped shower. The flow rate of an instantaneous shower is dependent on the temperature of the mains water supply.

Instantaneous gas water-heater An appliance that heats water on demand, whilst the water is passing through it.

Insulation resistance The effectiveness of the electrical insulation between current carrying conductors and earth.

Integrated power-showers *See* All-in-One Power-showers.

Kitemark Logo owned by the British Standard Institution, which indicates conformity to British Standards.

Level access Describes shower-trays that are installed so that any upward step into the shower is eliminated.

Lime-scale A build-up of alkali-based deposits formed from water flow, usually found in older pipework or tap bodies/shower outlets.

Low-level WC The cistern is fixed on the wall immediately above and behind the WC bowl and connected to it by a short flush-pipe.

MCB A miniature circuit breaker is an electrical circuit protection device used as an alternative to re-wireable and cartridge-type fuses. It trips out when too much current flows in the circuit, typically on fault conditions. Do not confuse with RCD.

Mains or water mains Refers to the cold-water supply delivered to the house by the local water company. This is clean drinking water (also called potable) that has been processed to remove any harmful elements. The original source of this water is a reservoir or pumping station and the water companies must supply water at an adequate pressure to get to the top of the building.

Mains pressure This is the pressure of the cold water supplied by the water mains. These pressures vary from location to location but only rarely is the pressure to a house lower than 2.5 to 3bar. A two-storey house with 'standard' 8ft (2.40m) ceilings and a header tank in the roof will only require the water to rise around 6 or 7m, which represents 0.6 to 0.7bar – so there is generally plenty of mains pressure. It is much more significant for high-level apartment dwellers, who may need to fit a booster pump.

Manual Mixing Valve A shower control which does not compensate for variations in the temperature or pressure of the incoming water supplies and needs to be adjusted manually.

Mechanical mixing valve Water fitting that requires manual operation to effect on/off flow control and mixed water temperature.

Minimum pressure The least pressure required so that a fitting performs adequately. Water pressure depends on the type of fitting and plumbing system installed. As a general guide, low-pressure systems are gravity fed and less than 1.0bar, high-pressure systems are mains-fed, pumped or combination boilers and are usually more than 1.0bar.

Monobloc mixer A single body fitting, requiring only one tap hole. Mixes water from hot and cold supplies, available in a basin or bidet fitting. Water can either be mixed in an internal chamber or at the point of discharge.

Mixer shower Usually refers to the mixer valve and the shower kit.

Modulating instantaneous gas water-heater An instantaneous gas water heater or boiler that is fitted with a gas-control mechanism to vary the heat input and produce a relatively stable domestic hot-water temperature, often termed fully modulating.

Multi-point An instantaneous water-heater that can supply water to more than one outlet, but not usually simultaneously.

Multi-panel folding shower screens Offer maximum protection against spray and folds neatly to the wall. They are ideal for smaller bathrooms or where you do not wish to see a permanent extended screen.

Negative head If the cistern is below the level of the shower-head, a gravity flow of water will not occur. A pump with special switching can be used to obtain a flow of water.

Non-rising spindle Non-rising headwork, handle does not rise it is opened to control flow.

Non-latching switch Identical to a bathroom ceiling light pull-cord switch, except that electrical contact is only made when the cord is being pulled.

Non-return valve *See* Check Valve.

Off-set corner bath Bath designed to fit into the corner of a bathroom with one side longer than the other, with the bathing area positioned parallel to the longer side.

Open outlet flow rate Maximum potential flow rate from mixing valve without shower fittings attached.

Outlet pump *See* Single Pump.

Overflow In washbasins there is usually an overflow beneath the highest level of the bowl, which drains into the waste outlet pipe, by-passing the plug/ mechanism.

Overflow (cistern) A pipe or device in a cistern that prevents water from overflowing by either internal means or via an external warning pipe.

Overflow warning pipe Pipe connected to a cistern to provide an early warning of an inlet-valve failure.

Pedestal washbasin A washbasin supported vertically by a column from the floor, designed to conceal pipe work with additional screws to fix it back to the wall.

'P'-trap Used to convert a horizontal inlet to a 14-degree fall (to wall) by the use of an outlet connector.

PCB Printed circuit board – a plastic board on to which a circuit layout to interconnect a number of electrical components is laid.

Parking bracket *See* Wall Bracket.

Performance standard Specification agreed between interested parties concerning the performance of a product under specified conditions, e.g. flow rate at a given supply pressure.

Pillar taps Separate hot and cold taps fixed to a horizontal surface, used to control on/off flow.

Pivot door A pivot door swings on two pins, located top and bottom within the door frame, they give a full-width look and open in a narrower space than hinged door.

Pop-up waste A lever to activate the operation of the plug in a bath or a basin negating the need for a plug and chain.

Porcelain-enamel A glazed finish produced by the application of a powdered inorganic glass either dry or suspended in water, to cast-iron parts, subsequently fused by application of high temperature.

Porcelain-enamel steel A coated steel tray pressed into shaped and sprayed with an enamel coating that is fired on at high temperature.

Positive head A volume of water held above the highest point on the system, allowing a flow of water through the pipework and out of the discharge point by gravity.

Potable water Clean water from the mains supply into the house that is used for drinking, heating, washing and toileting purposes.

Power-showers Power-showers have their rate of flow boosted with a pump. A bigger hot or cold water storage tank may be needed to supply the volume of water used by this type of shower.

Pressure accumulator A pressure vessel inside which is fitted a bladder to accommodate thermal expansion of water or alternatively to absorb the pressure shock waves of water hammer. Also known as expansion vessel.

Pressure-balancing mixing valve A pressure-balancing compensatory shower mixer valve designed to maintain a constant shower temperature under variable inlet pressures but maintained inlet temperatures.

Pressure-compensating *See* Pressure Balancing Mixing Valve.

Pressure-regulating valve Gives constant down stream pressure, irrespective of upstream pressure with built-in non-return valves.

Pressure-relief device Safety device fitted to prevent excessive pressure building up within an electric shower heater.

Pressure-relief valve Spring-loaded relief valve fitted to cold supply on unvented systems to relieve excess pressure safely to atmosphere.

Pressure switch A means of controlling the pump or other electrical equipment, by sensing a difference in pressure within the system.

Pressure test A test, usually associated with water supply pressures, to ensure no leakage at a specified pressure.

Primed Described the action of readying a component for use, usually by removing all of the air from the system/pump.

Pump hose A flexible pipe that connects the pump to rigid pipework.

Pump immobilizer A device to prevent the pump in a whirlpool bath from running without water (which will damage the pump).

Push fit connector Method of joining pipework components together with a push in type connector. Does not require brazing, sealant or adhesive.

Pushbutton The visible flush mechanism fitted to a cistern equipped with a flushing valve. A pushbutton is activated manually.

PVD A process performed in a vacuum chamber, which bonds the finish to the substrate of the tap.

Quarter-turn Refers to a tap with controls that move from off to fully open by turning through 90 degrees.

Rubber base-seal Rubber washer (elastomeric gasket) fitted between a tap and appliance to create a seal.

RCD A residual current device is an accurate electrical balance that measures the electrical loading on the outgoing live and return neutral conductors. If any current leakage exceeds the trip value under a fault condition it turns off the power supply. An RCD is sometimes known as ELCB, RCCB or trip switch. Do not confuse with MCB.

Recessed Refers to a shower-enclosure that is made up of a door that is set into an alcove made from walls – or could refer to a shower valve that is set into the wall. *See* Built-In.

Relay An electrical control device that uses a low voltage or current to operate a switch that can handle high currents and voltages.

Riser rail *See* Wall Bar.

Risers *See* Adjustable Legs. Also use to describe shower-trays that are fitted with adjustable legs.

Roll-top bath Freestanding bath, traditional in appearance with rounded profile to the top of the rim.

Running pressure *See* Dynamic Pressure.

'S'-trap Used to convert a horizontal inlet to a 14-degree fall (to floor) by the use of an outlet connector. The S-trap connector can also be turned to left or right to give a 90-degree turned P-trap.

Screed If a shower tray is being fitted onto a floor that is not flat or level, a layer of mortar or 'screed' must be spread evenly over the area where the tray is to be fitted. This will ensure that the floor is level.

Self-draining pipe work system (whirlpool) When not in use the system leaves almost no residual water in the pipework. There are degrees of self-draining.

Semi-countertop basin A basin that fits part-way into the countertop, leaving the front of the basin projecting and is held in position with the aid of clips and/or brackets.

Semi-pedestal basin Basin fitted with a pedestal to conceal supply pipes and waste outlet but the pedestal stops short of the floor.

Servicing valve A valve for shutting off the flow of water in a pipe connected to a water fitting to facilitate the maintenance or servicing of that fitting.

Shower-bath Bath designed to incorporate a shower, often provided with increased space and 'profiling' in the base for increased stability in the area intended for standing and showering.

Shower cabin A complete pre-assembled shower/steam room, usually consisting of overhead, hand and body showers.

Shower column *See* Shower Panel.

Shower controls Any device that supplies and controls hot- and cold-water supply for the purposes of shower-ing.

Shower curtain A waterproof curtain attached in front of a shower to contain the spray - suitable for most electric and medium flow-rate showers.

Shower-head A device that delivers the final spray or flow of water into the shower-enclosure – designed to produce a spray pattern.

Shower-hose A flexible pipe that connects between the shower-head and the shower control.

Shower kit A description of the components of a shower that is connected to the control valve – usually this is a shower-hose; shower-head or spray; wall bar with restraining device, and may also include elements such as soap dispensers.

Shower panel A pre-assembled shower unit consisting of one or more jets, requiring minimal installation. Wall-mounted, these units usually come with a variety of options ranging from thermostatic or manual mixing, with fixed overhead, flexible hand-showers and body showers, which can be manually or electronically controlled.

Shower temple A pre-assembled shower-enclosure with tray and usually incorporating overhead, hand and body jets. These units may also feature a steam function.

Side-panels The side-panel is used with a door to form a two-, three- or four-sided shower-enclosure. They usually come in fixed sizes but can be extended using infill panels.

Silicone sealant A commercial sealing compound used to create a water tight seal.

Single check valve Also known as a non-return valve.

Single flow A mixer tap in which the hot and cold water mixes within the body of the fitting. To comply with water regulations, such fittings require single check valves to be fitted to each inlet if the supply pressure is unbalanced.

Single lever Mixer using only one handle (lever) to control flow and temperature. Typically applied to monobloc or some two tap-hole mixer designs.

Standard dimension Dimension agreed as a convention, e.g. mixer tap holes for baths should be approximately 180mm (7.25in) apart.

Single pump A pump used for drawing water from a mixing valve for delivery to a shower.

Slidebar *See* Wall Bar.

Sliding door The sliding door is an alternative method of access when there is limited space in front of the enclosure, or within the enclosure, for a swinging door. They can be fitted to standard-sized enclosures and to larger oblong-type shower-trays ie: from 1200 to 2000mm long.

Solenoid valve An electrically operated valve giving either no flow or full flow.

Spa jet The device in the bath from which air is forced into the bath.

Squatting pan A WC that is mounted into the floor with only the top portion visible. The user 'straddles' by placing their feet either side of the bowl.

Static pressure The water pressure existing at a fitting when no flow is taking place.

Steel bath Bath formed from pressed sheet steel with a surface coated with vitreous enamel.

Stop-cock or **stop-valve** A valve used to isolate the mains cold-water supply to a building.

Storage cistern A cistern, other than a flushing cistern, which is used to store water for subsequent use.

Strainer A filter in the form of a mesh screen to prevent debris from entering a water fitting.

Supply pipe A pipe conveying mains cold water around the building.

Supply pressure Pressure measured at the inlet of a water fitting.

Syphon Device used for flushing WC cisterns. Syphons are operated by a lever and provide a flush by means of syphonic action. Syphons are fail-safe and cannot leak.

Syphonic flushing system Water flows into the bowl and at the same time a device lowers air pressure in the trap-page. Atmospheric pressure creates a syphonic action drawing any waste material through the trap into the drainage system.

Tap-body A cast housing that accommodates the head-work and hand-wheel or lever. Key attributes are the ability to deliver acceptable volumes of water and aesthetic appearance.

Tap connector Device used to facilitate connection of a tap's inlet tails to the hot and cold water supplies.

Tap headwork The switching mechanism within the head of a tap or water fitting that controls the flow rate and sometimes temperature.

Tapered baths Baths designed to optimize the use of space in a bathroom, usually narrower at the foot end.

Temperature- and pressure-relief valve A relief valve fitted to unvented cylinders to relieve excess pressure safely to atmosphere.

Temperature test Usually associated with thermostatic mixing valves. A test to establish that a safe, mixed-water temperature is not exceeded.

Thermal storage hot-water system A hot-water system where cold mains pressure water is heated (instanta-neously) as it passes through a heat exchanger surrounded by a stored volume of hot water.

Thermostat Temperature-sensitive device producing a linear or rotary motion to control the mixing of hot and cold water within a thermostatic mixing valve.

Thermostatic mixing valve A device to compensate for variations in the temperature of incoming water supplies, to maintain a selected mixed water tempera-ture. Also known as TMV.

Three-hole tap/mixer Typically a central spout and two separate handwheel controlled assemblies. The 'body' of the mixer is normally concealed beneath the exposed surface of the basin.

Touch pad control Electronic control that engages the functions of the system, i.e. intensity of bubbles, by pressing the Keypads.

Transformer An electrical device for converting mains voltage to low voltage.

Trap Pipe fitting or part of a sanitary appliance, that retains liquid to prevent the passage of foul air.

Twin pump Two pumps driven by a single motor, boosting both hot and cold supplies to a shower mixer and/or other terminal fittings. (Two pumps can be used in place of a twin pump.) Also known as twin-ended pump or twin impellor pump.

Two-way doors Two-way doors are ideal for both small and large openings. Such doors are extremely safe as access is gained by opening inwards or outwards.

Unbalanced pressure A term used to describe when water arrives at the tap from separate sources at different pres-sures, e.g. high pressure from the mains (cold) and low pressure from the water tank (hot).

Unvented domestic hot-water cylinder A plumbing system where the cold feed is taken directly from the mains to provide a high pressure hot-water supply. There is no open vent to atmosphere.

Up-stand Lipped area around the edge of a shower-tray, which is intended to fit behind the final wall finish to form a better water seal with the wall.

Upstream Water flowing towards a given point of reference.

Vent pipe An uninterrupted safety pipe that allows air or expansion of water within a hot-water system to escape to atmosphere.

Vessel basin A washbasin that has the appearance of a bowl that simply sits on top of a cabinet or a counter-top.

Wall bar A vertical rail-assembly that is part of the shower kit. The shower-head is usually fixed to the wall bar with an adjustable fixing that allows height adjustment of the spray.

Wall bracket Fixed device for holding hand-showers.

Wall elbow *See* Wall Outlet Connector.

Wall-hung WC A WC that looks as though it is hug on the wall, with no means of support from the floor. It is actually supported by floor brackets or by wall frames positioned behind the wall. The cistern is also out of sight, behind the wall.

Wall outlet connector Wall-mounted device to enable a flexible shower-hose to be connected to concealed pipework. Sometimes described as a wall elbow.

Warning pipe An overflow pipe positioned so that its outlet is in a conspicuous position so that the discharge can be readily seen.

Wash-down flushing system The modern method of flushing a toilet pan clean, in which the water cascades into the sump of the bowl, from around the rim of the pan, to flush away the waste material. This system is suitable for any type of building.

Waste pipe A pipe that takes waste water from a WC or washbasin into the drainage system.

Water fittings Includes pipes, taps, ferrules, valves, cisterns, mixing valves and similar apparatus used in connection with the supply of water within a building.

Water-jacketed tube heater *See* Thermal Storage Hot-Water System.

Wax capsule device A heat-sensitive component that is part of a thermostat. As variances in the heat causes the wax to expand or contract, the balance of hot to cold water flow is adjusted and the temperature of the water is kept constant.

WC Water-closet (WC) is a generic term used for all types of toilet.

Whirlpool jet Device for allowing air/water to enter the bathing area of a whirlpool bath.

Whirlpool pipework Either flexible or rigid, for conveying air/water to the jets in the bathing area.

Useful Addresses

Armitage Shanks
Armitage
Rugeley
Staffordshire
WS15 4BT

Tel: 01543 490253
www.armitage-shanks.co.uk

The Association of Plumbing and Heating Contractors (APHC)
This the leading Trade Association for the plumbing and heating industry in England and Wales. For a list of members telephone or visit the website.

Tel: 02476 470626
www.aphc.co.uk

Bathroom Manufacturer's Association
Federation House
Station Road
Stoke on Trent
ST4 2RT

Tel: 01782 747123
www.bathroom-association.org/

The Bathroom Manufacturer's Association (BMA) is the trade association that represents the major manufacturers of bathroom products, ranging from sanitaryware, baths, taps, showers, enclosures, accessories and furniture.

Fordham
PO Box 155
The Woodlands
Roysdale WayEuroway Trading Estate
Bradford
West Yorkshire
BD4 6ST

Tel: 01274 654700
www.fordham.co.uk

HansGrohe
Unit D1 and D2
Sandown Park Industrial Estate
Royal Mills
Esher
Surrey
KT10 8BL

Tel: +44 (0)870 7701972
www.hansgrohe.co.uk/

Ideal Standard
The Bathroom Works
National Avenue
Kingston Upon Hull
HU5 4HS

Tel: 01482 346461
www.ideal-standard.co.uk

The Institute of Plumbing and Heating Engineering (IPHE)
This is the UK's professional and technical body for all plumbing and heating professionals. All members listed have had to prove their competence through recognized qualifications or extensive experience, the prime objective of improving the science, practice and principles of plumbing and heating engineering in the public interest. For a list of members telephone or visit the website.

Tel: 01708 472791
www.iphe.org.uk

Thermostatic Mixing Valve Manufacturer's Association
This is concerned with TMVs and aims to ensure the safe provision of hot water at point-of use.
www.tmva.org.uk

Trevi Showers
The Bathroom Works
National Avenue
Kingston Upon Hull
HU5 4HS

Tel: 01482 346461
www.trevishowers.co.uk

Jacuzzi
PO Box 155
The Woodlands
Roysdale WayEuroway Trading Estate
Bradford
West Yorkshire
BD4 6ST

Tel: 01274 654700
www.jacuzziuk.com/

Kaldewei
Unit 7
Sundial Court
Tolworth Rise South
Surbiton
Surrey
KT5 9RN

Tel: 0870 777 2223
www.kaldewei.com/

Kohler Mira
Cromwell Road
Cheltenham
Gloucestershire
GL52 5EP

Tel: 01242 221221
www.mirashowers.com/

Scottish and Northern Ireland Plumbing Employers Federation (SNIPEF)
This is the trade association representing businesses involved in the installation and maintenance of plumbing and heating systems. For a list of members telephone or visit the web-site.

Tel: 0131 225 2255
www.snipef.org

Sottini
The Bathroom Works
National Avenue
Kingston upon Hull
HU5 4HS

Telephone: 01482 449513
www.sottini.co.uk

The Blue Book – Online
Ideal-Standard (UK) Ltd
The Bathroom Works
National Avenue
Kingston upon Hull
HU5 4HS

www.thebluebook.co.uk/

Mark Wilkinson
Overton House
High Street
Bromham Nr. Chippenham
Wiltshire, SN15 2HA

Tel: 01380 850004
www.mwf.com

Ripples
PO Box 136
Kingswood
Bristol
BS30 6YE

Tel: 0117 973 1144
www.ripples.ltd.uk/

Index

Acrylic baths 35, 38
Alcove enclosures 92, 94

Back-siphoning or back-flow 33
Basin and bath taps
  Bath/shower mixer-taps 70, 72
  Four-hole mixer-taps 71–2
  Monobloc mixer-taps 70–1
  Pillar taps 70–1
  Single-lever mixer-tap 68, 70
  Three-hole mixer-taps 71–2
  Two-hole mixer-taps 70–1
Bath shapes 39–41
Bathroom layouts - typical 17
Baths 35–48
Bidets 66–7
Brassware 68–77

Cast-iron baths 36, 39, 40
Cast-resin baths 37, 39
Check valves and isolating valves 73
Choice of tap-holes 65
Corner enclosures 92

Downstairs cloakroom 12

Electric showers 99–102

Fashion trends 9–10

Fault diagnosis for tap installations 77
Fitting instructions 33
Framed shower-enclosures 91

Gravity-fed water system (diagram) 25
Guide to installation 29
  baths 43–5, 48
  electric showers 104–8
  mixer showers 108–118
  shower enclosures and screens 95–8
  shower trays and panel 85–8
  taps and mixers 75–7
  washbasins 65–6
  WC pans and cisterns 56–8
Hand-rinse basins 62–3
High pressure hot water system with combi boiler (diagram) 27
High-pressure systems 24
Hot water storage capacity 27

Inclusive 42
Installing – see guide to installation

Legislation and standards 11, 128–31

Low-pressure systems 24

Minimum space requirements 18
Mixer shower valves 99–100, 102–4

Peninsular enclosures 94, 95
Physics of waste removal 30
Planning your bathroom 14
Plumbing systems 23
Pressure reducing valves 73
Privy 8
Pumped gravity water system (diagram) 25

Rate your bathroom 15–16
Readying the room 29
Restraining device 32

Safety and health 34, 45, 74, 98, 118
Sanitaryware 49–67
Sanitaryware construction methods 50–1
Shower-baths 41
Shower controls and kits 99–118
Shower-enclosure 89–98
Shower-screens 95
Shower-trays 78–88

Shower-trays – materials 78–80
  acrylic 78
  cast acrylic 80
  fireclay 80
  solid surface 78–9
  steel-enamel 79
Shower-trays types, shapes and sizes 80–3
Single-stack system (diagram) 31
Sources of supply 20–2
Spa baths 46
Specifying shower controls 104
Specifying shower-trays 83–4
Steel baths 35, 38
Stop valves or stop taps 23
Taps and water pressure 75
Tap-valve, ceramic disc 69
Tap-valve, rubber washer 69

Templates 66
Thermostatic mixing valve 28, 74
Tin Bath 9
Toilet Seats 61
Tools & equipment 34

Unframed shower-enclosures 91

Ventilation 29
Victorian roll-top bath 38

Walk-in shower-enclosures 91
Washbasins 61–6
  countertop basin 63
  pedestal basin 62–3
  semi-countertop basin 63–4
  semi-pedestal basin 62–3, 67
  under-countertop basin 63–4
  vessel basin 63–4

wall-hung basin 61
Water pressure 28
Water temperature 28
Water-closet cisterns 56
Water-closets 52
  back-to-wall wc 54, 60
  high-level wc 53
  low-level wc 52
  squatting pan 54
  wall-hung 54, 60
  close-coupled wc 52
Water-traps 55
WC cistern fittings 59
WC flushing operations 55
WC outlet types 55
Wellness or super-showers 92
Wet-rooms 92
Whirlpool baths 46